A SALUTE TO FETCHAM

THE STORY OF A SURREY VILLAGE IN WORLD WAR ONE

LYN ROZIER & JANICE STEELE

First published in Great Britain in 2018 by
LEATHERHEAD & DISTRICT LOCAL HISTORY SOCIETY
& MUSEUM,
64 Church Street,
Leatherhead
KT22 8DP

CONTENTS

ACKNOWLEDGEMENTS

PETER TILLEY
JEAN WILLIS
GOFF POWELL
SURREY HISTORY CENTRE
ANCESTRY
FIND MY PAST
LORRAINE SPINDLER
LEATHERHEAD AND DISTRICT LOCAL HISTORY SOCIETY
NATIONAL ARCHIVES
BRITISH NEWSPAPERS ARCHIVES
THE RED CROSS
LOST HOSPITALS OF LONDON
WORCESTERSHIRE REGIMENT
BEDFORD REGIMENT
PRESENT OWNERS OF THE WELL HOUSE

FOREWORD

LYN ROZIER

As a child, I was taken by my father every Sunday to see the Changing of the Guard at Buckingham Palace, followed by a walk in St. James's Park. I grew up with a love of marching bands and the military. I still remember visiting Westminster Abbey Field of Remembrance Day each year and watching my father sadly observe and remark on the poppy crosses planted for friends in The Queen's Royal Regiment killed in World War Two. This instilled in me a great respect for those men and with the anniversary of World War One I wanted to find out about the Fetcham men who sacrificed their lives and to make sure that they are not forgotten.

We hope that this book will give an insight into life in Fetcham in The Great War, as it was referred to and serve as a memory of those inhabitants of the village.

JANICE STEELE

In 1966, I went with two daughters to live in Combles, Northern France. We were there for three years whilst my husband worked for the Commonwealth War Graves Commission. We had two cemeteries in the village and when I felt homesick I would walk to them and read the names on the headstones and felt empathy for those men who died for their country and their families.

That time in France when the autumn came and the fields were ploughed a different way, artefacts would be unearthed and on long walks we would collect some of them. To this day two old bayonets are used for the garden line.

For many years, I have been researching my family history and joined a local history group and from that interest I produced two booklets one for World War 1 and a second for World War 2 about the men whose names are inscribed on our Fetcham War Memorial. I am actively researching further information.

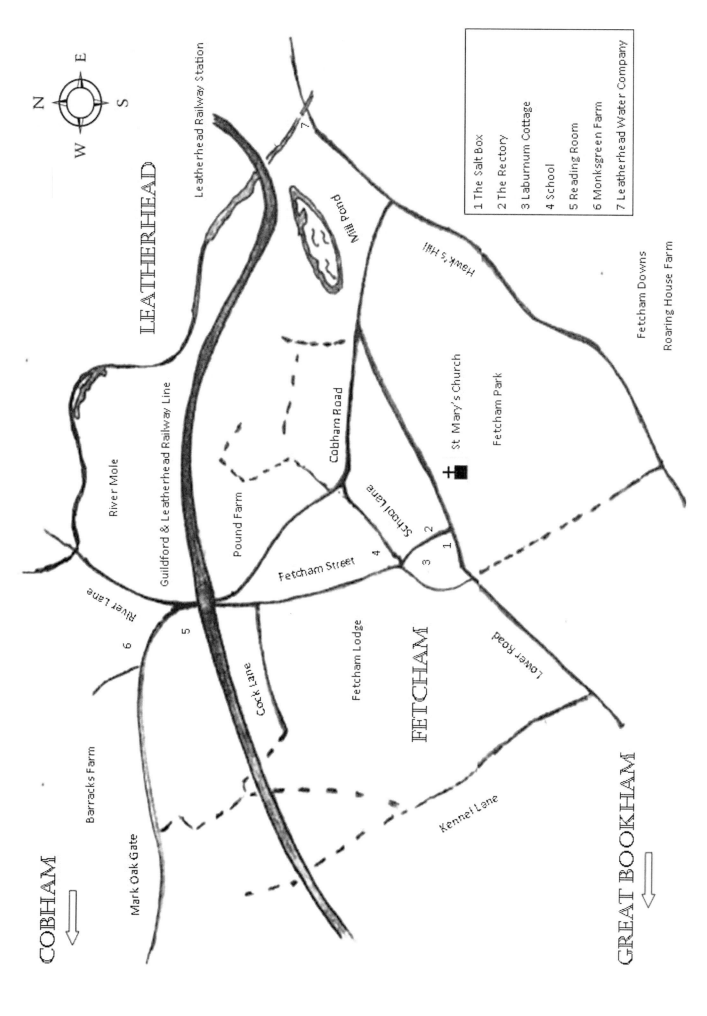

Key

1 The Salt Box
2 The Rectory
3 Laburnum Cottage
4 School
5 Reading Room
6 Monksgreen Farm
7 Leatherhead Water Company

LEATHERHEAD

COBHAM

FETCHAM

GREAT BOOKHAM

Leatherhead Railway Station

Mill Pond

Hawk's Hill

Fetcham Park

St Mary's Church

Cobham Road

School Lane

Fetcham Street

Fetcham Lodge

Pound Farm

Guildford & Leatherhead Railway Line

River Mole

River Lane

Mark Oak Gate

Barracks Farm

Cock Lane

Lower Road

Kennel Lane

Fetcham Downs

Roaring House Farm

5

CHAPTER 1

FETCHAM 1911 AND THE WAR YEARS

Many books have been written about the history of Fetcham but this book is about the period of the First World War 1914-1918 and the lives of the men, women and children in the Village.

Feccham (sic) was recorded in the Domesday Survey and prehistoric remains dating back to 4,000 BC have been found in the district along with three Saxon burial sites at Hawks Hill. Fetcham at the turn of the 20th century would have been a quiet rural village of around 400-450 inhabitants, bounded by the River Mole to the east and nestling between the town of Leatherhead, which had a population of roughly 5,500 residents and the village of Bookham, about three times the size of Fetcham. The village had a Mill but the death of the local Miller and Corn Merchant, Henry Moore in February 1915 brought its life to a close. The Mill itself was destroyed by fire in 1917. The Mill Pond would have covered a greater area than today coming to within a few yards of the Cobham Road.

The parish church of St Mary's is of early Norman style, and has a bell tower with three bells and a clock dial which was erected in 1897 at the time of the Diamond Jubilee of Queen Victoria. Two Rectors were to serve the community prior to and including the war years, John Dalyell Henderson and William Henry McKennal Caldwell.

The Alms-houses, contained six sets of rooms and were erected in 1886 and a Reading Room, on the site of the earlier alms-houses provided the village with its first purpose built meeting room and stands just beyond the railway bridge in Cobham Road going towards Stoke D'Abernon, in an area of the village known as Monk's Green.

The Fetcham Mill Fire of 22 August 1917

St Mary's Church, Fetcham.

Monk's Green 1909 showing The Reading Room on the left

John Charles Knowles was the Parish Clerk and village schoolmaster. The school, which was erected in 1854, had an average daily attendance of seventy-nine pupils. The Post Office, which originally stood on the corner of Sandy Lane (now The Ridgeway), was looked after by Samuel Friston, the sub postmaster.

Gas was supplied by the Leatherhead Gas and Lighting Company from its works in Kingston Road, Leatherhead and water was provided by the Leatherhead and District Water Works Company where Ernest Moy was the Engineer in Charge. Although the railway ran through the village, there was and is no Fetcham Railway Station. There were two public houses, The Bell where Sidney Lambert was the publican and The Rising Sun run by Josiah Prutton, still recognisable today although it now operates as a Chinese restaurant.

The Rising Sun (now Zen Garden, a Chinese Restaurant)

Fetcham Post Office – corner of Lower Road and Sandy Lane (now The Ridgeway)

The area was chiefly an agricultural farming community, the chief crops produced being wheat, barley and oats. John Barnard Hankey of Fetcham Park was Lord of the Manor and principal landowner. The local farms included Home Farm worked by John and David Lang and situated near the village hall in The Street, Monk's Green Farm with Arthur Smiles as the farmer, Barracks Farm in Cobham Road, Cannon Court Farm, one of Fetcham's oldest farms farmed by Francis Maxwell Thomson and Roaring House Farm situated on Fetcham Downs. Notable private residents were Sir Ernest Blake of Hawkshill, Oliver Campbell of Sunnyside, Charles Stanley Gordon Clark, Miss Malleson of Mark Oak, Arthur Marson of Fetcham Cottage, George Bernard Mitford and William Woods of The Saltbox.

The Salt Box 1903 which stands on the corner of The Old Street and Lower Road

The 1911 Census provides an insight of Fetcham around the time of the outbreak of the First World War three years later. There were just over four hundred inhabitants of the village, a quarter of whom were children under the age of thirteen. One hundred and seventy of these individuals were married, with ten widows and two widowers. Six residents were over the age of seventy and there was one eighty-year-old. Apart from agricultural labourers or farm workers, the inhabitants were mainly employed as servants or gardeners working in the larger properties, and included three chauffeurs, three butlers and two nurses. Also listed were six carpenters or cabinet makers, two blacksmiths (although one was retired), an Assistant Bank Manager and four clerks (two of whom were in Holy Orders). Around a fifth of the villagers gave their birthplace as Fetcham.

The Old Street 1906

The Parish Records for St Mary's Church revealed that during the four years of the Great War, thirty-two babies were baptised including the daughters of Arthur Bearsby the Gamekeeper and Sidney Lambert the Publican and James Alexander. Grace Friston the daughter of the Postmaster, Myra Lambert the Innkeeper's daughter and John Gravett's daughter Mildred were among the eleven marriages which took place. Nineteen burials were also performed, this number sadly included three children, one year old Peggy Penny and two five year olds, Archie Alexander and Bertha Nelson, whose funeral was recorded in the School Log books when the girls and infants class of the school attended. There were of course other souls lost from the village – the men who names are recorded on the Fetcham War Memorial and who are remembered in foreign soil.

When 1914 dawned, village life continued through the Spring and Summer – with local events being reported in the press - in May a concert was held in the Reading Room including songs by members of the Fetcham Choral Society under the direction of Mr H W Mills, their conductor, along with violin and pianoforte solos. A short play 'Time for Money' was also staged. The annual summer festival in connection with the branches of the Girls' Friendly Society took place at Fetcham Lodge in June, by kind permission of Mr and Mrs Gordon Clark 'with members numbering nearly two hundred and fifty assembling at Fetcham Church for a short service before adjourning to Fetcham Lodge

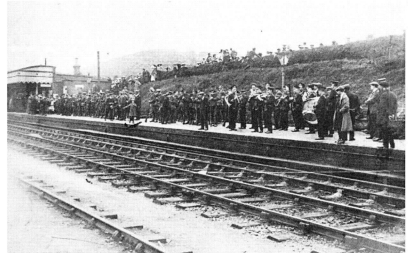

where tea and strawberries were provided in addition to musical programmes, games and walks in the beautiful grounds'.

By August the mood was changing and on 4 August 1914, Germany attacked France through Belgium, and Britain declared war on Germany. Men of the Dorking Company of the 5th Battalion the Queen's (Royal West Surrey) were mobilised and left Dorking station on Tuesday 5 August.

The 5th Battalion Queens (Royal West Surrey) Regiment leaving Dorking station 5 August 1914

Despite the declaration two more local events took place including the annual horticultural show, open to the cottagers of Great and Little Bookham, Effingham and Fetcham was held at Eastwick Park. The weather had been unusually dry but 'despite difficulties the exhibits reach a high degree of excellence' with 'the ladies' classes being extremely well patronised and adding considerably to the attractiveness of the show.' Mr Gravett, the gardener to Mr Gordon Clark of Fetcham Lodge 'showed a splendid collection of decorative roses', and 'Miss Smiles of Monk's Green showed some fine begonias', - and the 'annual fete and gala promoted by the Leatherhead Friendly Societies, in aid of the Hospital and Convalescent Homes was held at Fetcham Grove with an afternoon programme of sports with prizes kindly presented by the tradesmen of the town'.

Field-Marshal Lord Kitchener had issued his first appeal for volunteers on 7 August. He also permitted the part-time Territorial Force – originally intended primarily for home defence – to expand and to volunteer for active service overseas. After a relatively slow start, there was a sudden surge in recruiting in late August and early September 1914. In all, 478,893 men joined the army between 4 August and 12 September, including 33,204 on 3 September alone – the highest daily total of the war and more than the average annual intake in the years immediately before 1914.

The Defence of the Realm Act 1914 was passed on 8 August 1914 during the early weeks of the war and gave the government wide ranging powers, such as the power to requisition buildings and land needed for the war effort. Trivial peacetime activities were no longer permitted included flying kites, starting bonfires, buying binoculars, feeding wild animals bread, and discussing naval or military matters. Alcoholic beverages were watered down and pub opening times were restricted to noon – 3 pm and 6.30 pm to 9.30 pm.

The Battle of Mons signified the first engagement between British and German forces on the Western Front, and began on 23 August 1914. The tone of the local press began to change with recruitment notices, reports of casualties and advertisements reflecting wartime austerity. In September, the Surrey Advertiser began publishing a 'Call to Arms' as a regular feature followed by requests for 'Tobacco for our Soldiers'. Local Recruitment Centres were located in the Municipal Buildings, Leatherhead and Hook Road, Epsom.

The local people would have seen the opening of The Red House Auxiliary Hospital in Leatherhead on 21 October 1914, its first patients being wounded Belgian soldiers.

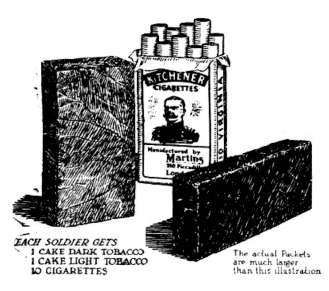

EACH SOLDIER GETS
1 CAKE DARK TOBACCO
1 CAKE LIGHT TOBACCO
10 CIGARETTES

The actual Packets are much larger than this illustration

The First Battle of Ypres began on 14 October and lasted until 22 November and the newspapers published an appeal for 'Christmas Boxes for All'. The first German air raid on Britain was carried out on 21 December. In November 1914, National Egg Collection was launched under the patronage of H M Queen Alexander with the aim of providing newly laid eggs to the wounded in hospital in Boulogne.

In December, the Dorking and Leatherhead Advertiser stated 'if only every person who keeps fowls in Great Britain and Ireland would promise a few eggs a week, the pressing need of our wounded can be easily supplied'.

Tobacco for our Soldiers – Dorking and Leatherhead Advertiser 26 September 1914

The customary Boxing Day meet of the Surrey Union Foxhounds at Box Hill was abandoned on account of the war, although the pack did meet on Boxing Day in the cricket ground near the Bell Inn– village life had changed – and for some nothing would ever be the same.

The Bell, Fetcham showing The Surrey Union Foxhounds

Research from the many thousands of service records that survive from World War 1 provides definite identification of over fifty local Fetcham people who served during WW1 either in the armed services or as voluntary aid nurses. These can be linked to other records that confirm their connection to family members and to the village and their stories are told in this book.

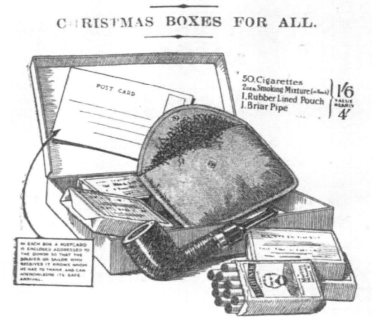

Our Soldiers and Sailors Christmas Boxes for All - Dorking and Leatherhead Advertiser 21 November 1914

The advertising of everyday commodities would now reflect the ongoing crisis such as the Paisley Flour advert which appeared in the Surrey Advertiser in April 1915 entitled 'Children's Joy – no need to deprive them of dainties in war time. Light and wholesome cakes with no heavy indigestible lumps and nothing in them but what you know is there are made cheaply with Paisley Flour', whilst Hudson's soap advert 'Billeted with Hudson's' read

'Tommy is the first to appreciate a clean Billet and the first to lend a hand to keep the Billet clean. He is, you may be sure, QUITE AT HOME, with Hudson's Soap. This good old soup is always of Uniform quality, so Tommy is perfectly equipped with it. A clean, sweet smelling wholesome soap, Hudson's ensures cleanliness with typical British Thoroughness. Tommy and Hudson's will both be busy this Spring. SPLENDID FOR WASHING UP AFTER MEALS'.

Sunlight Soap expressed their thanks to *'the Navy which enables the industries so vital to the country's welfare to still be carried on. The beautiful oils and tallow from which Sunlight Soap is made come from overseas – from Australia, the Islands of the Pacific, from the West Coast of Africa etc. Cleanliness salutes the Flag. It is our duty to transform every shipment of oils into perfect soap and thus endeavour to do credit to the Navy'.*

Hudson and Sunlight Soap advertisements

Bird's Custard advertisement Dorking and Leatherhead Advertiser May 1915

Bird's Custard advised 'not wasting crusts and stale bread but to use them to make a delicious Bread Pudding and serve it with Bird's Custard'. Their advert in the Dorking and Leatherhead Advertiser in May 1915 read 'Bird's Custard has the taste you all enjoy – it is an altogether good taste – a combination of freshness, niceness, purity and wholesomeness. The liking for it needs no cultivating! It comes naturally – even to young children. Grown up folk who thoroughly relish the Bird's Custard flavour – hearty men who never eat sweets etc. retain their boyish eagerness for Bird's the perfect custard'.

With the aim of saving paper and preventing surplus waste a notice in the Dorking and Leatherhead Advertiser in April 1916 read: 'Save the Paper – The government has restricted the output of paper. We are therefore compelled to save in every direction possible, and ask our readers to help. They can do it by giving a definite order to the Newsagents for the Dorking and Leatherhead Advertiser to be supplied weekly. Give your orders at once and so avoid disappointment'.
Dorking and Leatherhead Advertiser April 1916

FETCHAM.

SAVE THE PAPER.—The Government has restricted the output of paper. We are therefore compelled to save in every direction possible, and ask our readers to help. They can do it by giving a definite order to their Newsagents for the DORKING AND LEATHERHEAD ADVERTISER to be supplied weekly. Give your orders at once and so avoid disappointment.

Military supplies were advertised by Alfred Bull of Guildford and job vacancies stipulated that the male applicant must be ineligible for the Army or over military age or discharged from the forces.

ALFRED BULL
AND CO., LTD.,

22, High Street,
GUILDFORD.

MANUFACTURERS OF MILITARY WATER-PROOF SLEEPING VALISES, GROUND SHEETS, CANVAS KIT BAGS, CANVAS BUCKETS, POLE STRAPS, TRANSPORT COVERS, MILITARY & HOSPITAL TENTS, MARQUEES ALL SIZES, FLAGS FOR SALE OR HIRE.

Alfred Bull advertisement Surrey Advertiser 19 April 1916

WANTED. Blacksmith, able to do shoeing and heavy coach work; must he ineligible for Army; good wages to suitable man.—Apply Hall and Co., Croydon. Limited Brighton-road Redhill.   b377

WANTED. Boy or Girl, left school, who can cycle, to do a small country round.—Lee, Newsagent, West-street, Reigate.   a5848

WANTED in Reigate, at once, man over military age or discharged from Forces as Gardener, etc., and able to make himself useful and be able to clean motor; full or part time.—Apply with full particulars to Box 2505, Surrey Mirror, Redhill.   a5825

Surrey Mirror 1916

Beechams' Pills used the heading 'Both Booming' with' National War Bonds offering the security of Victory, and Beecham's Pills the security of Health' whilst the International Stores suggested 'Two Ways of 'Helping to Win' by buying War Bonds and drinking coffee for breakfast' - altering your breakfast 'taste' for the time being is not a great sacrifice, but it will enable the Food Controller to more easily cope with the present shortage of tea'.
Beecham's Pill advertisement Surrey Advertiser December 1917

BOTH BOOMING

NATIONAL WAR BONDS
The Security of Victory,
AND
BEECHAM'S PILLS
The Security of Health.

International Stores advertisement Surrey Mirror December 1917

Two Ways of "Helping to Win."

First—   Buy National War Bonds.

Buy as many and as often as you can. The greater your purchases of National War Bonds, the greater the comfort of the armies fighting for you; the greater the power of the offensive; the sooner will come the hours which will form the Peace Terms that you want. You can purchase National War Bonds at any Money Order or Post Office from £5 upwards.

Second—   Drink Coffee for Breakfast.

To alter your Breakfast "taste" for the time being is not a great sacrifice, but it will enable the Food Controller to more easily cope with the present shortage of Tea. You can purchase at the International

Delicious Pure Coffee 1/6 and 1/8

International Stores
THE BIGGEST GROCERS IN THE WORLD
TEA :: COFFEE :: GROCERIES :: PROVISIONS

Save your Money.
Help the State.   Earn Interest.
Prepare for the Future.
BUY WAR SAVINGS CERTIFICATES
at any Bank or Post Office.

It is your duty to save a little money week by week and by so doing help yourself and the State at the same time. NOW is the time to begin. Act on the impulse. You will always be glad that you did. Your Local War Savings Committee or Association will give you full particulars.

Issued by the National War Savings Committee
(Appointed by His Majesty's Treasury),
Salisbury Square, London, E.C. 4.

War Savings Certificates Surrey Mirror October 1917

Beef tea was advertised in January 1918 the advert reading 'Don't worry about food – Economy in food is a National necessity. A less amount of food must be consumed. You need, therefore, more nutriment from the smaller quality – you need Jardox – the real beef tea with the real beef flavour.'

Jardox Beef Tea advertisement Dorking and Leatherhead Advertiser January 1918

CHAPTER TWO

A SCHOOL LOG BOOK– THE KNOWLES FAMILY AND MISS BALLARD

JOHN CHARLES KNOWLES

John, a school master and Parish Clerk, was born in Darwen in the Blackburn area of Lancashire in 1859. His father Simon was a Rent Agent, and his mother Alice was a Heald Knitter, a type of weaver. In 1861, they lived at Bank Top Cottages, Over Darwen.

The 1881 Wales census showed John as a twenty-one-year-old student at the College Road Training College, in Carmarthen. Ten years later the 1891 census confirmed that thirty-year-old John had followed his chosen profession and had become a school master, lodging at Lower Freystrop, Haverford West, Pembrokeshire where he taught at the local school.

The Summary of HM Inspector's Report for Freystrop School for the same year showed John was the Certificated Teacher. The Inspector's report read 'the Elementary work was on the whole good, but the character of the Reading, Recitation and Writing and the Mental Arithmetic admit of improvement. English was fair, and Geography pretty good. The Infants did well. The prepared needlework was pretty good, and the exercises fair. The singing by note was pretty good'.

Summary of H. M. Inspector's Report on the School.

"The Elementary Work was on the whole good, but the Character of the Reading, Recitation and Writing, and the Mental Arithmetic admit of improvement. English was fair, and Geography pretty good. The infants did well. The prepared needlework was pretty good, and the exercises fair. The singing by note was pretty good."

Master of School – John Charles Knowles. Certificated Teacher of the II.d Class.

National School Admission Registers and Log-books 1870-1914

Two years later, on 28 December 1893, John married Elizabeth Jones at All Saints, Tufnell Park, Middlesex. Their daughter Jessie was born in 1895 in Carmarthen, followed three years later by the birth of their son Robert Cecil in Pontardulais, Llanelly.

The family moved to Surrey and in 1901 the census records showed that John had become the Head Teacher at Fetcham Village School, with his wife Elizabeth also teaching there. Apart from his school career John also served for many years as the Parish Clerk.

Both of their children attended the school as pupils although Robert moved to Dorking High School in September 1911 as a Day Scholar and left on the 17 November 1913. His occupation to be taken up on leaving school was given as 'at aeroplane works.' The Fetcham School Log Book recorded daughter Jessie being taken by her father John for an interview at Wallington High School on 5 March 1917.

John was the Head Master of Fetcham School throughout the period of the First World War but he did not live to enjoy a long life in peacetime. A School Log book entry showed that he was in hospital at Guildford and was visited by his wife on 29 November 1921. The entry for the following day, 30 November reads 'Mr Knowles, Head Teacher of this school died this morning. Mrs Knowles will remain away until after his funeral.' He was buried in St Mary's Churchyard on 3 December. He was 62 years old.

His wife Elizabeth ceased work at the school in June 1922 and a new Head Teacher, a female, Kathleen Cheyney took up her role at the start of the new school year on 4 September, when she was joined by a Miss Violet Madge who was appointed as a student teacher

ROBERT KNOWLES

Robert's interest in aircraft made the Royal Flying Corps a natural choice for him to serve with during the conflict of World War One. At the start of the War the Royal Flying Corps was the air arm of the British Army and it consisted of five squadrons, four aeroplane squadrons and one observation balloon squadron, first used for aerial spotting on 13 September 1914.

Royal Flying Corps Cap Badge. The Royal Flying Corps motto was 'Per ardua ad astra' (Through adversity to the stars). This remains the motto of the Royal Air Force (RAF) and other Commonwealth air forces.

Initially, their main objective was to carry out photographic reconnaissance but as the war progressed they carried out bombing raids on military and industrial targets, and would have been involved in dog fights with German aircraft, doubly dangerous as no parachutes were available throughout the war. Robert's military record showed that he became a 2nd Lieutenant and was hospitalised on the 22 May 1918.

Robert married Annie Victoria Chapman on the 4 February 1922 at Leatherhead Parish Church.

The Royal Flying Corps class being given instruction on the rotary engine (Royal Air Force Museum)

Robert was twenty-three, three years older than his bride Annie. They gave their address as Motor Works, Kingston Road, Leatherhead.

Royal Flying Corps poster

Havilland DH4 of 31 Training Depot Station, Fowlmere, 1918

Further service records show that he attended a De Havilland Civilian Flying School re-qualifying course from the 28 May to 2 July 1923, followed by annual training in 1924. He also trained at Brough C. Flying School for sixteen days where is it recorded that 'he was rather slow in picking up the feel of this machine but improved towards the end of the course and eventually flew well'.

His mother Elizabeth was to pass away in 1927 and was buried with his father John in St Mary's, Fetcham. The Electoral Roll for 1939 showed that Robert continued in his flying career and was listed as a Flying Officer in the Royal Air Force. The couple's address at this time was given as Rose Cottage, Chertsey Road, Woking. He died in September 1984 in Surrey, at the age of 86.

ALICE VICTORIA BALLARD

Alice was the Infant School Teacher at Fetcham Village School throughout the war years. She was born in Wandsworth on 12 September 1879 and the 1891 Census showed her living at Gilbert Road, Wimbledon with her family. Alice was eleven at this time with an elder sister sixteen-year-old Louise and fourteen-year-old brother Edwin and younger brothers and sisters nine-year-old Henry, seven-year-old Byron, four-year-old Maud and baby sister Violet.

In 1894 Alice was a pupil at the Haydon's Road Church of England School in Wimbledon and a note in the school log book dated 22 October indicated that 'Alice Ballard, who has been doing duty as Monitoress, from this time, will be a Candidate for 1st Year.' In 1900, nearly a quarter of the teaching profession were pupil-teachers and they were by far the largest source of recruitment to elementary schools. In 1900 regulations for pupil-teachers changed increasing the minimum age to fifteen except where Her Majesty's Inspector authorised an earlier age, usually in rural areas. To be accepted, they must be approved by an HMI, pass a medical exam and pass an examination set by the Board of Education in Reading and Recitation, English, History, Geography, Arithmetic, Algebra, Euclid (boys) or Needlework (girls), and Teaching. Pupil-teachers were not allowed to teach more than five hours a day or 20 per week although in some areas this did vary. They were examined annually by HMI. When their term of service was completed they could sit the Queen's (King's from 1901) Scholarship exam. A 1st or 2nd class pass in this qualified the holder to enter training college although it didn't guarantee it as applicants were far more numerous than places. According to *History in Education* (University of London), by 1900 barely 44% of eligible pupil-teachers were accepted'.

On May 3 1895, the Reverend A M Pickering wrote 'Alice Ballard has not given satisfaction in the discipline of her class this week, she has been told that a great improvement must take place'. There was disappointment for Alice in September 1895 when a note in the log book read 'Alice Ballard's parents do not wish her to be a teacher; therefore, her indentures were not signed'. Alice left the school on the 27 September 1895.

Haydon's Road School Log Book September 1895

However, it appeared Alice was able to fulfil her ambitions and did indeed become a teacher. In 1901 Alice and her family are shown at living at 19 Norman Road in Wimbledon. Her fifty-seven-year-old father Edwin Ballard's occupation was given as a Cellar Man and her sister Louise was now employed as a dressmaker. Twenty-one-year-old Alice was described as an Assistant Teacher and her brother Harry worked as an Apprentice Printer whilst Byron was employed as a Junior Clerk.

She commenced teaching at Fetcham Village School as a thirty-one-year-old Supplementary Teacher on the 1 February 1910 when the school log book referred to her as 'late of Great Totham School, Essex' where presumably she had been a teacher.

Mixed classroom of young children with their teacher, circa 1900.

The 1911 Census confirmed the family continued living at Norman Road, Wimbledon. Her brother Edwin had now become a house painter and Harry a Compositor, whilst Byron was described as a Manufacturers Assistant Agent-Woollens. Some three years later, in February 1914, the Fetcham School Log book revealed that Alice had been granted a week's leave from School owing to the death of her sister Maude, who was subsequently buried in Merton.

The school Log Book dated April 23 1915 recorded the celebration of St George's Day at the school, when a new poetry book 'Richard ll' was introduced to Class 1. It also referred to Alice as being 'absent in the afternoon with a headache'. The children suffered many outbreaks of infectious diseases such as Mumps, Measles, German Measles and Chickenpox and in October 1916 Alice herself was absent from school suffering from a septic throat which meant that the older girls from Upper Standard would take it in turns to take the Infants Class. One little five-year-old boy pupil was diagnosed with Diphtheria and sadly died some days later on the 29th.

In May 1916 Alice was granted leave to see one of her brothers off to the Front. On 14 December, the Infant children's school work was examined, the Headmaster, Mr Knowles recording in the Log book as follows:

'very fair progress can be reported in numbers, reading and writing and very good in recitation. The order is not as good as formerly and there is a lack of cloakroom supervision. Miss Ballard absent today – mother ill.'

In September 1918, he wrote 'heard Miss Ballard give a lesson on 'The Blackberry' to infant's class. The class seemed very backward and dull.'

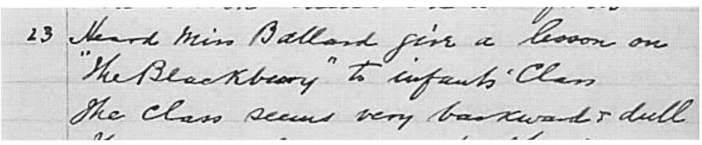

Fetcham School Log Book 23 September 1918

Alice took leave on the 7 and 8 November 1918 to meet her brother on his return from France. After the war, it appeared that Alice suffered bouts of ill health and absence and attended St Thomas Hospital on 2 November 1923 to see a specialist and the Log of the 9 November referred to her being 'called to enter hospital for an operation' with two children from Class I helping with the work of the Juniors and Infants in her absence. On the 12 November 'Owing to Miss Ballard's absence the Time Table has been adapted to meet present conditions and several alterations have been found necessary. Class I girls have assisted in the Infants Room today'.

Fetcham School Log Book November 1923

She finally left teaching at Fetcham School in June 1925.   The School Log Book dated 30 June noted the following: 'the timetable was interrupted at 3 pm in order for a presentation to be made to Miss A V Ballard. Miss Ballard ceased duties here this pm.'

Alice was never to marry and until the Sex Disqualification Removal Act was passed in 1919, no married women had been allowed to work as teachers. The act should, in theory, have meant greater equality for women entering the profession, but in the 1920s, working women were frowned upon as there were so many unemployed men. The authorities used 'marriage bars' to prevent married women working as teachers. This rule meant that if a woman teacher married, she had to resign from her job; if she was already married, she was sacked. Some women found a way around the marriage bars by marrying in secret and then living apart from their husband, or by having a very long engagement.

In September 1930 at the age of forty-nine she was to pass away at the South London Hospital, Clapham Common, leaving her estate to Mary Elizabeth Ballard, a Widow.

A SCHOOL LOG BOOK

In 1854 land was donated by the Hankey family for a new Church of England school in Fetcham, which opened with sixty-one children on the register, each paying a penny a week to attend. Although the school building has had many alterations over the years, it is still easily recognizable from old photographs and stands on the corner of The Street and School Lane.

Fetcham School 1904.

Fetcham School 1910. Mr Knowles on the left.

The School Log Book was the Head Teacher's daily record of activities and they were obliged to be kept from 1862 onwards. The Fetcham Log entries showed new children joining the school, the school leavers, attendance records, notes on infectious childhood diseases, medical visits by doctors and the school nurse, progress and inspection of school work, weather conditions, lessons, comments on teachers and a mass of miscellaneous comments. The following are in some cases direct quotations from the School Logs Book and written as found.

Cover and inside page Fetcham Village School Log Book 1900-1914

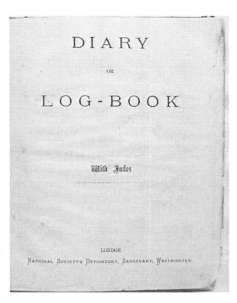

Autumn Term August 1914

The new school year began at the end of August, with low attendance due to the rainy weather. Much had changed, on 1 August Germany had declared war on Russia, and followed by declaring war on France and invading Belgium and on 4 August Britain itself declared war on Germany. No reference to the war was made in the Log Book until 15 September when no woodworking class was held as the teacher, Mr Hurford at Leatherhead Centre, '*had enlisted on the 43rd day of the war with Germany*'. Unfortunately, on 23 September 'the gardens were entirely denuded of plants by Mr Lang's cows which entered by breaking through a fence', but all was not lost as the Rector presented the school with 500 spring cabbage plants on 2 October.

School Log Book September 1914

In October pupils visited Randalls Park, the occasion being an inspection of the Public Schools Corps by His Majesty the King, a terrestrial globe was presented to the school and there were further references to gardening lessons and nature walks which indicated the importance placed on growing plants and a general understanding of nature in a mainly agricultural area. In November, the Tuesday timetable was modified for the Winter with the boys of Upper Class having cardboard modelling from 10-12 am, followed by drawing in the afternoon, and the younger boys clay modelling from 1.30 to 2.15pm. The girls had sewing classes from 2.35 to

3.55pm, whilst Arithmetic was on the agenda for the Upper Standards, with the Lower Standards studying Reading and Composition.'

School Log Book 27 November 1914

The Infants Class work was examined and 'satisfactory progress found to have been made, the class being happy and industrious'. The headmaster examined the work of the Upper Class on 23 December and noted 'very fair progress, although the papers were not as neat as formerly.' The Rector and Miss Henderson regularly visited the school and invited the children and teachers to tea in the schoolroom on the 31 December when the infants 'gave a very pretty little play entitled 'The Months' in a very engaging manner'.

January 1915 started with heavy snowfall and low attendance; however, the school received a good report from the Diocesan Inspector: 'The school was inspected just a week after the Christmas holiday. The knowledge shown by the children generally and their interest and intelligent answering speak well for the careful instruction which must have been given during the year. I was particularly pleased with the practical grasp which the two upper groups displayed with regards to the catechism. The recitation was creditable and the written work good'.

In March the gardening class recommenced but there were no woodwork or cookery classes for the children as the Leatherhead Centre was occupied by the military. Mrs Gordon Clark and Miss Henderson visited the school and the girls sang 'The Battle Hymn' conducted by Mrs Gordon Clark who presented the school with the 'Land and Water Map of the War'.

The school reopened on 12 April after the Easter break and the following day 'the girls attended laundry lessons at the Leatherhead Centre whilst the boys went to woodworking. The garden class was held as usual in the morning.' St George's Day was celebrated as was Empire Day when the flag was hoisted and saluted and the pupils sang 'The Union Jack' and other songs. No visitors were invited however owing to the war.

Empire Day 1913 in Woking - Reproduced by permission of Surrey History Centre

The School, with a weekly average of fifty-nine children closed for the summer holidays on 21 July and 'the Rector presented a large framed Roll of Honour to contain the names of old scholars who were serving their King and Country in the Great War'.

Autumn Term August 1915

By August huge losses of life and injuries had been encountered, and the initial patriotic enthusiasm had waned. The absence of many of the men now serving in the forces was having an impact on local communities, with concerns over manpower available for the harvest. The children would now have been familiar with seeing troops training locally and wounded soldiers returning.

The School re-opened on 23 August and on 20 September the meadow fence was broken by an oak bough and Mr Lang's cows from Home Farm in The Street were again 'causing trouble having broken into the school gardens and doing much damage'.

Home Farm in The Street, Fetcham

In October, the children learnt 'La Brabanconne' the Belgian National Song, and Belgium refugees were now living in Leatherhead. By December a new song 'God bless the Prince of Wales' had been taught and the Standards could sing the national songs of six nations. The infants' class and Miss Ballard were examined in drill and she received her drill certificate and The Rector, Reverend Henderson, took his leave of the school on leaving the Parish. The final notation dated 22 December 1915 stated: 'The school was very nicely decorated with holly and mistletoe and a second donation of 10/-d. was collected from the children and had been sent to the Overseas Club. The School Roll of Honour now contains thirty-seven names'.

1916 dawned and school reopened on 10 January with Notice being given by the Surrey Education Committee to the Managers to consider a reduction in staff owing to the war, with the proposal that the staff be composed of the Head Teacher and one uncertified teacher. Miss Ballard was given provisional notice to be ready to be transferred to some other school. The Diocese Inspection took place on the 17 January with sixty-nine children present and Mrs Bernard Hankey and Mrs Townsend, Lady Managers and the Reverend C J Vernon, the Rector of Little Bookham present. A copy of the Diocese report read as follows: 'The teachers have evidently taken great pains over the religious instruction. The lessons have been well prepared on the right lines, the interest of the scholars has been aroused and maintained and the general knowledge shown is very creditable. The Upper Class did particularly well, showing a sound practical grasp of the order and main teaching of the Holy Sacraments. The Recitation as a whole was good. The written work was very good in the middle division and fairly good in the upper.' The new Rector of St Mary's, Reverend Caldwell made a visit to the school and on 21 January HM Inspector examined 'the Reading in the Infants room, and the Mental Arithmetic, Reading and Dictation and Composition of the older pupils. There had been a heavy fall of snow that day and only twenty-two children attended in the morning and twenty-four in the afternoon, although lessons were given as usual'. Early March saw more heavy snow and the school closed from 8-13 March until the snow had cleared. Another visitor to the school was Mrs Hankey 'who allowed the children to inspect the Cross of the Legion of Honour awarded to her son for bravery in leading a bombing party.' (see separate story and Worcestershire Regiment). The children had suffered from outbreaks of Mumps and Measles throughout the term which closed with reports of progress and term examination results sent to each parent.

After the Easter break the children commenced the term's lessons on the metric system, with more reports of Mumps and Measles. Thirty-six children were supplied with silkworm eggs for home rearing. The school celebration of Empire Day on 24 May commenced at 11.00 am with sixty-eight children present who sang the 'Children's War Hymn', 'Where go the Ships?' and 'Boys of the Empire League', whilst the Infants joined in with 'Soldiers and Sailors

Boys of the Empire' and 'Mine is the Country'. The children then gathered round the flag for the singing of the National Anthem'.

It was not until after the death of Queen Victoria, who died January 1901, that Empire Day was first celebrated on 24 May 1902, the Queen's birthday. Although not officially recognised as an annual event until 1916, many schools across the British Empire were celebrating it before then. Millions of school children from all walks of life across the length and breadth of the British Empire would typically salute the union flag, sing patriotic songs and listen to inspirational stories that included such heroes as Clive of India, Wolfe of Québec and General Gordon of Khartoum, but the real highlight of the day for the children was that they were let out of school early in order to take part in the thousands of marches, maypole dances, concerts and parties that celebrated the event. In the mid 1960's Empire Day became known as Commonwealth Day and in 1977 the date changed to the second Monday in March, when each year The Queen sends a special message to the youth of all the various countries of the Commonwealth.

By the end of May there were thirty children absent as Mumps broke out again and some children were kept at home for fear of infection and on 2 June the school was closed for three weeks owing to the epidemic. At the end of the month Mr E J Duffield of the Surrey Band of Hope visited the school and 'gave a very interesting lecture on beverages accompanied by chemical experiments.' The start of July was very wet with low attendance and thirteen-year-old William Lewer and twelve-year-old Wallace Tyrrell were 'excused attendance while they are employed in agricultural labour'. Gardening classes continued although unfortunately 'the garden did not appear so trim as usual owing to the school closure and much seed had failed'. Conscription had been introduced by the Military Service Act in January 1916 and by June this included married men, except those who were widowed with dependent children. Initially, Fetcham as an agricultural village would have seen farm labourers being allowed exemption but this was to change to satisfy the need for more men to serve at the Front. The first day of July 1916 had seen 19,240 British soldiers lose their lives, the bloodiest day in the history of the British Army.

Autumn Term 1916

School reopened after the summer break and Miss Ballard is taken ill with a septic throat and John Alexander is taken to Cuddington Isolation Hospital suffering from Diphtheria and the family excluded from school. Sadly, at the end of October the Log Book recorded that John had died. The Rector gave regular scripture lessons on Tuesdays and Thursdays and two young sisters were excluded from school suffering from Ringworm. The Christmas holidays commenced on 21 December with each pupil being given the customary report on conduct and progress to take home to parents.

School re-opened in January 1917 and received 6lbs of wool for the children to make into mittens and scarves for the soldiers. The weather was extremely cold towards the end of the month, with the temperature in the main school room only reaching 40 degrees. The Diocesan Inspection Report of 1 February stated 'the lessons have been well prepared, and were, in general, well remembered in spite of the Christmas holidays. The general bearing of the lessons was well grasped and the teaching had been reverent and practical. Recitation and written work very satisfactory.' The very cold weather and heavy fall of snow on the 5 February resulted in only thirteen of the sixty-nine children being present and the school was closed for the day. The school commenced with the War Saving scheme, which were introduced in 1916 to help finance the cost of the war and were regarded as the patriotic thing to do with villages and schools setting up schemes to encourage savings.

The Rector gave his usual lessons and as the severe weather continued, physical exercises were taken indoors. On the 27 February, the boys were able to attend the Leatherhead Centre for woodworking class and 'the girls and infants attended the funeral of Bertha Nelson late of the Infants Class'.

War Savings Advertisement *Dorking and Leatherhead Advertiser 17 November 1917*

The following day the school gardens were re-opened and Mr Budd and twelve boys commenced work on the plots, with four other unregistered boys commencing work on the big plot.

Nurse Watson arrived on the 22 March to inspect seventy children for cleanliness, three being excluded from school until the following Monday and five children cautioned for verminous scalp. Under the Education (Administrative Provisions) Act 1907 School Boards could act against parents who sent children to schools in 'verminous condition'. The war had an effect on the education of children and after the Easter break, two thirteen-year-old lads, Wallace Tyrrell and Edward Lewis left to work on the farms. From 1915 boys, and later girls, who had reached the age of thirteen might be excused further attendance at school to help on the land. Over one thousand, four hundred children in Surrey left school early under this scheme. The School War Savings Association Registered No. 184/102 Scheme 3 Accounts were audited by Mr Smiles, for which twenty-five Savings books had been issued, and four certificates bought. The sum of £4 1s. 11d. had been collected. Mr Smiles the Auditor, kindly added 6d to each book.

On 18 May, some fourteen children were absent with Measles in their homes and many more absent for fear of infection. Only twenty-seven children attended school on the 21 May when Mr Winter, the HM Inspector visited at 9.40 am. 'The following is a copy of a letter to the correspondent from the Medical Officer: 'You are under some misapprehension, as you speak of 'the epidemic of Measles! I have had no notification of cases of Measles in Fetcham. There have been a few cases of German Measles, an unimportant minor ailment for which closure of a school should be necessary only under the most exceptional circumstances. The School Attendance Officer states in a letter to me that the refusal of parents to send their children to school, is a matter with which he should deal, as there is no justification for their taking this course. I am unable to advise that the closure of the school is necessary. Signed J Williamson, Medical Officer, Epsom, 19 May 1917.'

The school closed for its Whitsuntide holidays on 25 May but there were no outdoor celebrations for Empire Day apart from hoisting the flag as there were only forty pupils present. The infants sang 'Patriotic Posies' with the Standards singing 'There's a Kingdom of the Seas'. No invitations had been given out but The Rector and Mrs Caldwell and several parents were visitors. The school prize winners were - in Needlework: First prize, Ivy Wakefield who received a wicker work basket containing scissors, thimble and reel of cotton, Dolly Parker second prize, who also received a wicker work basket containing thimble and reel of cotton (but no scissors were included in her prize) and third prize went to Maud Moore, who received just the wicker work basket, presented by Mrs Caldwell. The boys received prizes for Drawing, the first prize went to Ronald Lambert, second to Robert Mitchell and the third prize was awarded to James Butcher, - each boy received 'a handsome penknife', a gift from Mrs Caldwell. On 5 June, the Caravan Mission Van arrived in the village and the Mission Tent was erected in School Meadow until the Mission left on 18 June. The school closed on 1 August with further prizes being given to Nellie Cowan who left to attend Wallington High School and fourteen-year-old Francis Reeves who was leaving school.

Autumn Term September 1917

By now food supplies were running low and imported foods had become very expensive with food rationing being introduced in December. The final term of 1917 started on 3 September with sixty-six children present, but unfortunately 'difficulties were experienced in the arithmetic lessons in Upper Standards as the text books were worn out' and the children were once again succumbing to sickness in this case Chickenpox.

Mr B G Mitford presented the school with a coloured print 'Wreck of the Lusitania' the British Ocean Liner, which had been torpedoed by a German U-boat, in May

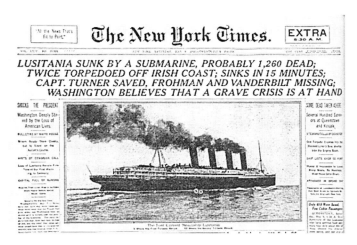

1915 eleven miles off the southern coast of Ireland with the deaths of one thousand, one hundred and ninety -eight passengers and crew and caused a huge public outcry both here and in the United States).

YPRES ANNIVERSARY.

Tribute to Colonel Hankey.

The third anniversary of the battle of Ypres was celebrated at Fetcham Schools on Wednesday morning, among those present being Mr. and Mrs. C. S. Gordon Clark, Mrs. Barnard Hankey, the Rev. W. H. and Mrs. McK. Caldwell, etc.

Mr. Gordon Clark, in an address to the children, said that at the battle of Waterloo in 1815 it was the thin red line which saved Europe and civilisation from the domination of Napoleon, and 99 years after, at the first battle of Ypres, it was the thin khaki line which saved France and England and the whole of civilisation from the domination of the Germans. Mr. Gordon Clark read an account of the battle by a writer who was present, who emphasised the work of the 2nd Worcesters in retaking the village of Gheluvelt, which saved the line. What was of special interest to them was that the Worcesters that day were led by a man who was born and bred at Fetcham. Writing of the affair that morning the "Times" said:— "We have been asked again and again why the General who saw the danger and gave the order was mentioned while the officer who led the battalion was unnamed. The battalion on that occasion was led by Major (now Lieut.-Colonel) E. B. Hankey, who happily still survived, and we trust the battalion will be awarded some special commendation, and that their leader will not be forgotten."

Proceeding, Mr. Gordon Clark said they were thankful that Colonel Hankey was still doing good work for them, and he was sure everybody would feel a real, consuming pride that it was he who led the battalion on that occasion. He suggested that a telegram should be sent to Colonel Hankey and the officers and men of the 2nd Worcesters, offering them hearty congratulations for their glorious share in that engagement.

This suggestion was carried out, and three cheers were given for Colonel Hankey, the proceedings closing with the singing of the Marseillaise and the National Anthem.

Thirteen-year-old drawing prize winner Robert Mitchell left school for farm work at Home Farm.

After the mid-term holiday the Anniversary of 1st Battle of Ypres was commemorated at the school and the *Surrey Advertiser* of 7 November 1917, carried an article entitled *Ypres Anniversary*.

In October, the Log described how Mr Budd, the so aptly named gardening tutor, had transferred three apple trees, which had been budded and grafted as lessons by the horticultural class, from the seed bed in the gardens to a site near the tool shed. A School Manager's Meeting was held on 29 October and appointed Mr Gordon Clark as Chairman and Mr William Smiles as Correspondent. These appointments were necessitated by the Rector leaving the Parish for service in Egypt as an Army Chaplain. The Infant school was examined in December with the following observations: 'very fair progress can be reported in numbers, reading and writing and very good in recitation. The order is not as good as formerly and there is a lack of cloakroom supervision'. Another calendar year was drawing to an end and 14-year-old Ronald Lambert left, along with Frank Alexander who had passed his Labour Examination and was presented with 'Under Wellington's Command' in appreciation of his help as Senior Monitor. Each child was given a report on their progress and conduct during the term

By early 1918 school attendance nationally was at an all-time low with repeated outbreaks of Diphtheria, Whooping Cough and Measles amongst the children and the teachers themselves became ill as the general health of the nation declined. Schools were forced to close for weeks at a time. When Fetcham School reopened in January there was a poor attendance due to an outbreak of Whooping Cough, and just nineteen pupils attended school on 17 January which resulted in Dr Williamson making several visits and finally advising on the 30 January that the school be closed until 25 February.

With food shortages, the garden class undertook the cultivation of an estate plot adjoining the school gardens and were assisted by ten boys from Class II who are not on the garden register. When the school broke for the Easter holidays, it was noted 'the three-week closure earlier in the term and low attendance had greatly affected the work of the school'. Two children left to continue their education at senior schools, Vera Shuffill to attend Surbiton High School, and Sidney Osbourn to Guildford Grammar School. Empire Day was celebrated but illnesses took hold in July with twenty-four children being absent on the 1 July and thirty cases of Measles being reported to the Medical Officer on the 3 July when only thirty-four children attended school. The following day, 4 July Dr Williamson, the Medical Officer for Health at Epsom advised the closure of the school again, to re-open on the 2 September.

Autumn Term September 1918 came around and a medical inspection of 5 and 6 year olds took place. On the 13 September Class 1, in response to an invitation from the Leatherhead Food Control Committee went blackberrying on Bookham Common and 48 1/2lbs of fruit was gathered and sent to the Food Controller at Leatherhead. Six days later the Upper Class went blackberrying, this time to Bookham Woods which resulted in 53 1/2lbs. of fruit being picked. ' Mr Winter, HM Inspector then visited the school and urged further efforts in blackberry picking and the Upper Class went to The Downs to pick more blackberries, with 30 1/2 lbs. collected on this occasion'.

BLACKBERRIES WANTED. — The Leatherhead Food Control Committee have made arrangements to meet the wishes of the Ministry of Food that the blackberry crop in the district should be gathered and sent to the jam factories for preserving. All who possibly can are asked to co-operate in the work, and payment will be made by the committee at the rate of 3d. per lb. for blackberries brought to the local Food Office, Church-street, between the hours of 5 and 7 in the evening.

Dorking and Leatherhead Advertiser 17 August 1918

In October Mr Dixon, the Attendance Officer gave notice that two thirteen year old boys, Jack Lambert and Fred Gravett, were allowed to do agricultural work for Mr Lang at Home Farm, and they were sent off potato picking and on 15 October Maud and Ethel Isted were also absent, potato picking. On 1 November Jack Lambert was re-admitted to school.

The school Log Book for the 11 November contained the stark entry 'Victory of the Allies – Surrender of Germany – signing of Armistice'. Throughout the war years there had been virtually no mention of the war itself in the Log Books.

The Rector Reverend Caldwell visited the school in mid-December on home leave from his duties in Egypt and the school closed on 20 December so bringing to an end the war years of the pupils, with peace declared and hopes for a happier and brighter future. A further entry in 1919 read: '19 July (Saturday) Celebrations of Peace throughout the country. In this Parish, the celebrations took the form of a procession in fancy dress round the lanes at 3 pm, a tea and sports for the children at 4, a dinner for returned soldiers at 6 and a dance in the school room (owing to rain) at 7 pm.' Mr Knowles, the wartime Headmaster, died in 1921 three years after Peace was declared and Miss Ballard after a period of ill health died in 1930.

One of the patriotic songs, the children sang at Fetcham Village School during the conflict was *God Bless The Prince of Wales,* written by John Ceiriog Hughes to celebrate the marriage of Edward VII to Alexandra of Denmark.

Among our ancient mountains
And from our lovely vales,
Oh! Let the pray'r re-echo,
God Bless the Prince of Wales!
With heart and voice awaken
Those minstrel strains of yore,
Till Britain's name and glory
Resound from shore to shore
Among our ancient mountains,
And from our lovely vales,
Oh! Let the pray'r re-echo,
God Bless the Prince of Wales!

Should hostile bands or danger,
E'er threaten our fair isle,
May God's strong arm protect us,
May heav'n still on us smile!
Above the throne of England
May fortune's star long shine!
And round its sacred bulwarks,
The olive-branches twine.
Among our ancient mountains,
And from our lovely vales,
Oh! Let the pray'r re-echo
'God Bless the Prince of Wales!'

27

CHAPTER THREE

THE RECTORS OF ST MARY'S AND CHRISTIAN MISSIONS

JOHN DALYELL HENDERSON

John was born 9 January 1857 in Jersey, Channel Islands. His father, Reverend William George Henderson, was a School Master and Clergyman from Hampshire, was thirty-seven years old at the time and his Scottish mother Jane, was twenty-nine.

John Dalyell Henderson

The Very Reverend William Henderson (1819–1905), First Headmaster of Victoria College, Jersey.

John was the eldest of fourteen children, having seven brothers and six younger sisters. Brothers and sisters Augustine, Ralph, Rosalie and Percy were all born in the Channel Islands, whilst Kate was born in Walmer in Kent and Wilfred, Charles, Harold, Constance, Robert and Muriel were born in Yorkshire where the family were shown in 1871.

John was educated from 1877 to 1881 at Queen's College, Oxford being awarded a Batchelor of Arts in 1881 at the age of twenty-four. The 1881 Census lists him as an Undergraduate Student at Oxford, but living at the family's address, the Grammar School, Leeds, where father William is a 'Clergyman without care of souls'. The household also included a domestic cook, a housemaid and a kitchen maid. From 1882 to 1884 John lived in Portsea, Hampshire, before going to Carlisle then moved to York in 1887 where he remained until early 1890 when he came to Fetcham and was listed in the 1891 Census living at Rectory Cottage, Fetcham.

His younger brother Wilfred died in 1896 in the Temperance Hospital, St Pancras. In 1901 John lived at Churchill Cottage, Portchester as a Church of England clergyman, his mother passing away in September of that year and his brother George died some eighteen months later in March 1903. Two years later his father died in September 1905, aged eighty-six.

The 1911 Census showed John with an older sister Mary living at Fetcham Rectory where he presumably lived until the new Vicar, Reverend Caldwell took up office in May 1916. The school log books for this period indicated the John and his sister were much involved with the village school, visiting it on a regular basis, checking the registers and giving scripture lessons and reviewing the work of the children and presenting prizes to the students. On 16 October 1912, according to the United Grand Lodge of England Freemason Registers, John was invited to a meeting at Leodride Lodge, Leatherhead.

The School Log Book entry for 14 May 1914 referred to the Rector visiting the school 'in the afternoon and giving a lecture on 'Trinidad', illustrated by numerous specimens of vegetable and mineral production. The Rector has recently returned from a visit to the West Indies. The Upper Class have written an account of the lecture. '

> **252**
>
> 14 May — The Rector visited the school in the afternoon and gave a lecture on Trinidad, illustrated by numerous specimens of vegetable and mineral productions. The Rector has recently returned from a visit to the West Indies. The upper class have written an account of the lecture.

School Log Book May 1914

An extract from the Dorking and Leatherhead Advertiser dated 25 September 1915 gave a report on John's impending resignation from his Parish duties. 'At the morning service at the Parish Church on Sunday last, the Rector (Reverend J.D. Henderson) announced that owing to ill-health he would be shortly resigning the living of the Parish.

> **FETCHAM.**
>
> IMPENDING RESIGNATION OF THE REV. J. D. HENDERSON.—At the morning service at the Parish Church on Sunday last, the Rector (Rev. J. D. Henderson) announced that owing to ill-health he would be shortly resigning the living of the parish. The Rev. J. D. Henderson has been rector of the parish since the death of the Rev. Sir Edward Graham Moon in 1904, and is held in the highest regard in the parish, having always been most solicitous for the welfare of his parishioners. He is chairman of the Parish Council, and also represents the parish on the Epsom Board of Guardians and Rural District Council, while formerly he frequently played cricket for the village team. Latterly ill-health has troubled the Rector very much, and a long sea voyage some time since does not appear to have had the desired effect. The living of Fetcham, which is of the net value of £460, with a modern rectory, is in the gift of the executors of the late Sir Francis Graham Moon.

The Reverend J D Henderson has been rector of the parish since the death of the Reverend Sir Edward Graham Moon in 1904, and is held in the highest regard in the parish, having always been most solicitous for the welfare of his parishioners. He is chairman of the Parish Council and also represents the parish on the Epsom Board of Guardians and Rural District Council, while formerly he frequently played cricket for the village team. Latterly ill-health has troubled the Rector very much, and a long sea voyage some time since does not appear to have had the desired effect. The living of Fetcham, which is of the net value of £460, with a modern rectory is in the gift of the executors of the late Sir Frances Graham Moon.

Dorking and Leatherhead Advertiser 25 September 1915

On leaving Fetcham John returned north and according to Freemason records joined the Border City Lodge, Carlisle on 9 November 1916. John died aged sixty-two on the 27 November 1919 at Croft House, Heads Nook, Cumberland. His estate was left to his sister Mary Henderson, a spinster and his brother Charles Ferdinand

Henderson; Rear Admiral (retired) HM Navy. Effects £276 3s.3d. When brother Charles subsequently died in 1935 he left his estate to his sister Kate Henderson, spinster and Ralph Anstruther Crompton Henderson, a Colonel in HM Army. His estate amounted to £990 0s. 8d.

WILLIAM HENRY MCKENNAL CALDWELL

William was born in 1866 in St Kilda, Australia and was the son of Gavin Ralston Caldwell and Frances Jane (nee Wolseley). By 1871 his mother was a widow living on 'Interest of Clergy 'with the children, Brenda, Ina, Ralston, Etheline, William himself, and three-year-old Enid at Copse Hill, Wimbledon. The household also included a butler, nurse, housemaid and cook. Twenty years later in 1891 William was shown with his mother, now aged fifty-five living at Frimley, with a cook, a parlour maid and a housemaid. Both were living 'on own means'.

He married Jesse Elizabeth Oxley on 15 July 1896 at St Peter's Church at Mancroft in Norfolk and in 1897 their son Gavin Ralston Mure was born in Margate. By 1901 William, a clergyman, had moved to Bagshot, where they lived with a cook, a nurse for three-year-old Gavin and a housemaid/parlour maid. The family appeared to move around the country and by 1911 were living at the Vicarage of St Augustine's in Charlotte Street, Bristol, where William was a *'Clergy in Holy Orders'*.

His story unfolded with the aid of archived newspaper articles, the first being from the Dorking and Leatherhead Advertiser of 6 May 1916 which read as follows: 'The institution and induction of the Reverend W H McKennal Caldwell to the incumbrancy of Fetcham took place last week at the Parish Church of St Mary's.'

Red Cross records show that from January to September 1917 William also acted as Chaplain at The Red House Auxiliary in Leatherhead, with weekly services and occasional visits. *The Surrey Advertiser* dated 17 November carried an article which read 'The Reverend W H McKenna Caldwell the representative of Fetcham on the Epsom Rural Council has been selected to go as Chaplain to the Egyptian Expeditionary Campaign, having to report to Alexandria this week. He is expected to be away for two years, and during that time will be excused leave of absence from the Council.'

William's voyage was eventful: 'On the 30 December 1917, the Troopship SS *Aragon* arrived at Alexandria Harbour, having sailed from Marseilles on the 17 December. She was laden with around 2,700 troops bound for the conflicts in Palestine.

SS *Aragon (www.bedfrdregiment.org.uk)*

SS *Aragon* sinking with one of the lifeboats in the foreground (www.bedfordregiment.org.uk)

As she arrived in a convoy bound for the port, the rest of the ships sailed onwards to Alexandria and she lay up ten miles off shore, awaiting her escort. The 9,588 tons of ocean liner drifted gently as she waited within sight of land but was torpedoed by the German submarine and minelayer, the *UC-34*. The destroyer HMS *Attack* dashed to her rescue as well as every available ship within reach as she quickly sunk. Many of the men were fortunately rescued and taken onto the HMS *Attack* and had just stripped their oil drenched clothes from their bodies and laid on the deck when devastatingly she too was torpedoed by the same submarine, almost blowing her in two.

HMS *Attack* Source: www.bedfordregiment.org.uk

The following day, New Year's Eve, just as the rescue was called off, fleet auxiliary craft HMS *Osmanieh* also hit a mine in the area, taking another 197 soldiers and nurses down with her. Six hundred and ten of the two thousand, seven hundred passengers on board the HMS *Aragon* were lost at sea, including twenty-five of the new draft bound for the 5th Battalion of the Bedfordshire regiment.'

The Dorking and Leatherhead Advertiser dated 16 February 1918 ran the following article: 'The Reverend W H McKenna Caldwell, Rector of Fetcham was on board the '*Aragon*' when that vessel was recently torpedoed in the Mediterranean. Some time since the Rector volunteered for service as an Army Chaplain, and after a period of service in France was on his way to Egypt. When the vessel was torpedoed Reverend W H McKenna Caldwell managed to get on a raft, and being a good swimmer afterwards swam off, and brought two men on to his raft. They were later picked up by a mine sweeper and even then, had an exciting time in an encounter with a U boat. After being landed at Alexandria the Rector was confined to hospital for some time suffering from exposure'.

ON THE "ARAGON."—The Rev. W. H. McK. Caldwell, Rector of Fetcham, was on board the "Aragon" when that vessel was recently torpedoed in the Mediterranean. Some time since the rector volunteered for service as an Army Chaplain, and after a period of service in France was on his way to Egypt. When the vessel was torpedoed Rev. W. H. McK. Caldwell managed to get on a raft, and being a good swimmer afterwards swam off, and brought two men on to his raft. They were later picked up by a mine sweeper, and even then had an exciting time in an encounter with a U boat. After being landed at Alexandria the rector was confined to hospital for some time suffering from exposure.

William's wife Jessie must have been shocked by the news concerning her husband but 1918 was to bring further distress when their son Gavin was killed in action on the 9 October 1918, whilst serving with the Coldstream Guards with both The Cheltenham Chronicle of 5 October 1918 and the Surrey Advertiser reporting his death. William himself died on the 12 October 1926 in Norwich aged 60.

Dorking and Leatherhead Advertiser 16 February 1918

MISSIONS

The Church Army's caravan visit to Fetcham was recorded in the 1911 Census. Although it was parked in Stoke Road, the home address of the two evangelists was given as 55 Bryanston Street, London, the Church Army Headquarters. One of the young men was twenty-eight-year-old Samuel Leonard Heal from Devon and he was accompanied by a twenty-one-year-old assistant.

The use of vans and caravans came about when it became clear that the Church Army missions were rarely reaching people living in the countryside so in June 1892 the first mission van left London for more rural areas. Initially these vans were pulled by horses but later became motorised. They would visit different villages and take services in schools and open air meetings. Up to the beginning of World War One the Church Army also ran eight seaside missions and a letter in The Spectator dated June 1911 appealed for donations to 'The Church Army Fresh Air Homes' where mothers and children struggling with poverty could enjoy a fortnight's holiday in the fresh air and sunshine and plentiful food. However due to hostilities these now had to be closed down.

'The Church Army's aims were to provide working men evangelists and mission sisters to aid the clergy in parochial rescue and slum work and labour homes for outcasts and destitute men, women and children'. During World War One its resources were diverted towards the needs of service men both home and abroad running recreational huts, tents, hostels, rest homes, mobile canteens and visiting injured troops in hospital. The recreation huts in particular provided hope and light in the darkest of situations, and at their peak saw 200,000 men through them in a day, where they would find tea and biscuits, a space to read or play games, writing paper and spiritual support, as well as space for quiet reflection.' (The Church Army).

THE CHURCH ARMY FRESH-AIR HOMES.
[To the Editor of the "Spectator."]

Sir,—I venture to ask if you can find space for a humble appeal to your readers on behalf of the Church Army Fresh-Air Homes— an appeal from hundreds of mothers and children in the depths of proverty, who find in these Homes the opportunity of a holiday by the sea or in the midst of green fields for which they would otherwise long in vain. We send mothers with their children, thus giving to many an overtired mother freedom to take much-needed change and rest, with the added pleasure of her children's presence, and without the anxiety of what is to become of the children while she is away. £2 2s. will give two weeks' holiday to a mother and three children at our Homes at Bexhill, St. Leonards, or Godstone. Is it a great sum to ask? Surely not. If friends could only see the delight of our guests at finding themselves for a while among surroundings so different from their homes in London back streets, and could watch them improving in looks and health during their fortnight's stay in fresh air and sunshine (with plenty of good food, for many of them are more than half-starved), we know that we should not have to ask in vain. May we, then, beg for a prompt and liberal response to this humble cry from careworn mothers and ailing children cooped up in London when all the world is thinking of holiday-time?

Cheques will be most gratefully received by Miss Walker, Hon. Secretary, Fresh-Air Department, Church Army Headquarters, 55, Bryanston Street, Marble Arch, London, W., and should be crossed "Barclays, a/c Church Army," payable to Prebendary Carlile, Hon. Chief Secretary, or Mr. W. F. Hamilton, K.C., Hon. Treasurer.—I am, Sir, &c.,
W. CARLILE,
Hon. Chief Secretary.

The Spectator, June 1911

Samuel Heal married Alice Stirling Jack in Kingston in September 1911 and later served with the Army Service Corps Reg No DM2/178638 although it is unlikely he went overseas. Samuel died suddenly in 1915 aged thirty-three, and was buried in December 1915 at All Saints Church, Kingston. His funeral was reported in the local press as follows: 'The funeral of Captain Samuel Leonard Heal of the Church Army, whose death occurred suddenly at a meeting of St Paul's Band of Hope, Kingston Hill on Wednesday evening last week, took place on Monday afternoon at Kingston Cemetery being preceded by a service at St Paul's Church. The large congregation was representative of religions and social work in the district. The Reverends E S Shuttleworth (vicar) and P J Coleman officiated and the singing was led by the St Cecilia Choir. Among those present in church were Captain Harrison representing the Church

Army headquarters and Captain A C Glover representing The Depot, East Surrey Regiment and Mr Bashford of the London City Mission'. Samuel was posthumously awarded the Victory and British Medal.

The Caravan Mission van visited Fetcham again on 5 June 1917 and the Mission Tent was erected in School Meadow where it remained from 5 June until the Mission left on 18 June, its presence being noted in the school log books. Similar work was carried out by The Salvation Army and the Open-Air Mission amongst others.

The Open-Air Mission produced a booklet priced at 1d. which included hymns and prayers and offered the purchaser 'an Active Service New Testament for free if the recipient promised to read and keep it'. They also offered a pen pal service whereby a 'Christian lady or gentleman would gladly write to a service man at the Front or elsewhere so that he may never feel he was without a friend'.

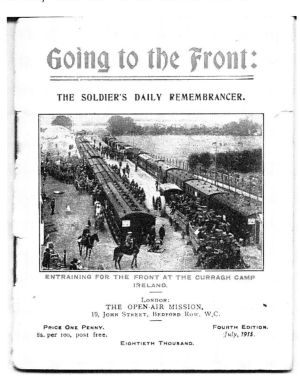
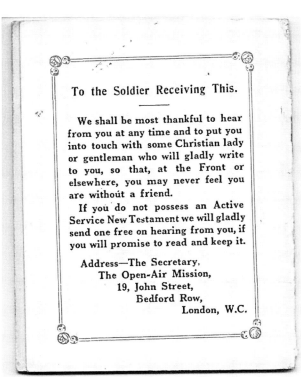

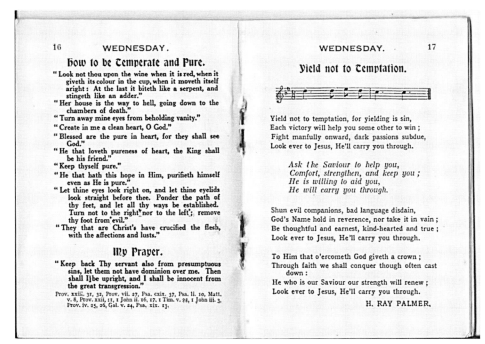

Pages from the Open Air Mission Booklet of 1915

CHAPTER FOUR

CONSCRIPTION AND TRIBUNALS

The Military Service Act of 27 January 1916 brought conscription into effect for the first time in the war. Every British male subject who:

- on 15 August 1915 was ordinarily resident in Great Britain and who had attained the age of nineteen but was not yet forty one and

- on 2 November 1915 was unmarried or a widower without dependent children, unless he met certain exceptions or had met the age of forty one before the appointed date, was deemed to have enlisted for general service with the colours or in the reserve and was forthwith transferred to the reserve.

Under Section 20 of the Reserve Forces Act 1882, The Admiralty had the first right of call on men who expressed a preference to join the Navy. Men were encouraged to voluntarily enlist under the Group System (Derby Scheme) before the Act came into place. There were four grounds for exemption:

i. if it is expedient in the national interests that he should be engaged in other work, or, if he is being educated or trained for any other work, that he should continue; or

ii. if serious hardship would ensue owing to his exceptional financial or business obligations or domestic position; or

iii. ill health or infirmity; or

iv. conscientious objection to the undertaking of combatant service.

False statements or misrepresentation at time of application for exemption could lead to imprisonment with hard labour for up to six months. In May 1916 conscription was extended to include married men and the age limit was lowered to eighteen. Conscripted men now had no choice about which service, regiment or unit they joined. Clergymen, teachers and some classes of industrial worker were exempt and included coal miners, and doctors. Men who felt they should be exempt from the draft due to poor health, potential damage to their business, family hardship or a conscientious objection had to apply to a tribunal, which would decide whether or not they should be conscripted. Many farming families, who were struggling with lack of labour, went to tribunal to try to get their sons exempted from service, though not always successfully.

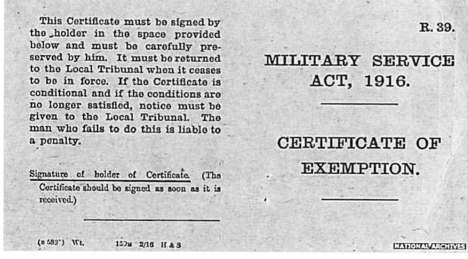

Certificate of Exemption – Military Service Act 1916

Those who were exempted from military service were issued with papers and badges to prove they were undertaking war work. Several of these badges were officially produced and distributed nationally but many more were produced privately by employing companies to support their employees. After conscription, the need for these badges faded, along with the white feather campaign. However, many continued to be worn throughout the war, especially by female shift workers for whom the badge could give priority boarding and fare concessions on public transport, as well as indicating that there was nothing disreputable about these ladies travelling alone at night.

Local Military Tribunals

HENRY ADDISON - Home Farm, Fetcham – Absentee

According to the Dorking and Leatherhead Advertiser, 15 April 1916. 'At the Epsom Petty Sessions on Monday, before Mr R Braithwaite and other magistrates, Henry Addison (20) labourer of Home Farm, Fetcham was charged with being an absentee under the Military Service Act, on April 8th. Prisoner pleaded guilty. PC Lewis said on April 8th, he received an Army form to make inquiries respecting prisoner. He knew he was at work at Home Farm, and proceeded there and found prisoner. Witness showed him the Army Form and asked him why he had not joined the Army or reported himself. He replied '*I have been discharged*'. He asked prisoner for his discharge papers when he replied, '*I have not got them. To tell you the truth I have not been up*'. He then took prisoner to the Leatherhead Police station – Sergt. Evans, recruiting officer at Leatherhead, said prisoner was called up on March 4th, the notice being issued to him on February 19th. Prisoner failed to report himself. The Chairman said the Court could impose a fine, but they were not going to do that. Prisoner would be handed over to the Military escort, and they hoped he would be a good soldier.'

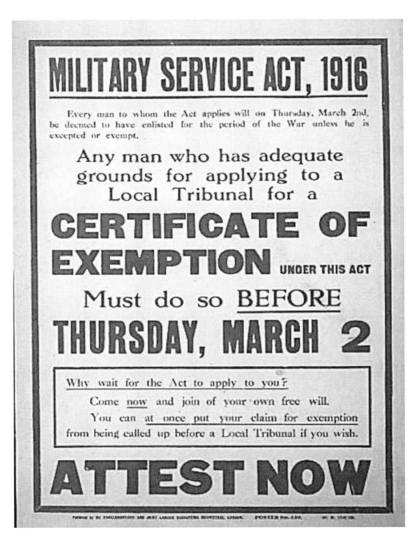

Military Service Act 1916 poster

JOSPEH COWAN - Waterworks, Fetcham. Epsom Rural Tribunal. Case Adjourned.

Adjourned:—Ernest W. Lofts. Barnett Wood-lane, Ashtead, dairyman; A. F. Goddard. 2, Smallholdings, Ewell, market gardener; Francis W. Hales, Meadow Walk, Ewell, insurance agent; J. P. Clark, Holland-avenue, Cheam, jockey; Harry W. Fuller, High-street, Cheam, hairdresser; Herbert S. Hicks, London-road, Ewell, commercial traveller; Francis T. Morris. 5, Cottage-road, West Ewell, grocers' assistant; J. J. Cowan, Waterworks, Fetcham; F. Kilburn, Stoke-road, Fetcham, endrive driver; Ernest E. Moy, Waterworks, Fetcham, works manager; G.

Joseph, whose father was a tinsmith, gas fitter and plumber, was born in Egremont, Cumberland in 1880. In 1911 Census Joseph lived at 2 Inkerman Terrace in Leatherhead. He had been married for seven years to his London born wife Helena and they had four daughters, Nellie aged six, five year old Hannah, Joyce aged three and Grace who was seven months old, the two younger girls being born in Fetcham. He was employed as the Superintendent of the Waterworks.

Surrey Advertiser 12 July 1916

The original Leatherhead and District Water Company Works.

The first works of the Leatherhead and District Water Company opened on 11 October 1884 and stood between Waterway Road and Bridge Street close to the present day waterworks. The Works 'consisted of a well two hundred feet deep, a steam-driven pumping station and a covered reservoir on high ground to the edge of the town. At an elaborate ceremony at the opening of the Waterworks it was pointed out that the new system at Leatherhead adjoined that of the Lambeth Water Company near Esher so there would be ample opportunity for the Leatherhead company to sell much of its water to London'. These original Works were demolished in 1992 to enable the building of the apartments overlooking the River Mole in Wallis Mews.

The Fetcham School Log Book for 3 July 1914 revealed Joseph and Helena's daughter Joyce had been *'re-admitted to school at the beginning of the week but left before the end as her parents objected to lessons being taken out of doors'*. In early 1918 a female doctor, Dr Boyes examines the children at Fetcham school but the youngest of the Cowan children, Mary 'is absent owing to her parents objecting to the medical examination'. A medical examination of the five and six year old pupils took place in September and 'Mary was inspected on her own, resulting in a letter of protest from Mr Cowan'.

At the beginning of the War, the Special Constabulary was ordered into a body similar to the present day one: a voluntary, part-time organisation, paid only their expenses.   Its primary function was to prevent German infiltrators from interfering with the nation's water supply.

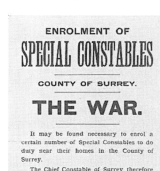

ENROLMENT OF

SPECIAL CONSTABLES

COUNTY OF SURREY.

THE WAR.

It may be found necessary to enrol a certain number of Special Constables to do duty near their homes in the County of Surrey.

The Chief Constable of Surrey therefore requests that all loyal persons (not under 21 years of age) who may be willing to serve in the capacity of Special Constable, will give their names to the nearest Police Constable of the district in which they reside.

M. L. SANT, Capt.,
Chief Constable of Surrey.

Advertisements for Special Constables appeared requesting men to give their names and addresses to the nearest police station. They had to be in good health and over twenty one years old and Joseph, who was now in his mid-thirties, was one of those to apply.   Leatherhead had forty one Special Constables who were sworn in at the Council Offices by a Mr A H Tritton and the Reverend St Clare Hill.   Most would have been engaged in other forms of employment and went on duty throughout the night. Joseph was one of the men.

The *Dorking and Leatherhead Advertiser* reported on the 12 September 1914 that 'the special constables of Leatherhead are still engaged in guarding the waterworks and reservoirs of the town. One Monday afternoon Mr J Cowan who is a special constable saw a well-dressed man making a sketch of the L and R W R bridge which spans the River Mole. Mr Cowan's suspicions were aroused, and he took the man to the Leatherhead Police station. Enquiries were made and the stranger was soon able to establish his identity as a London Council school teacher, who was on holiday and was following his hobby of sketching'.

So that's what you've joined, is it! Who are you that you should think you can keep law and order?

Joseph also served as Chief Fire Officer of Leatherhead Fire Station. An article in the Dorking and Leatherhead Advertiser of 26 September 1914 reported that' at the meeting of the Fire Brigade Committee it was resolved that Mr Allen be appointed chairman of the committee during Mr Gregory's absence on active service. The Chief Officer (Mr J Cowan) reported that Firemen Weller, Skelton, Worsfold and Batchelor were now serving with the colours, and recommend that Messrs Boorer, J May, A Ayling and B Smallpiece be appointed members of the Brigade during the absence of those on active service'.

After the war, the Electoral Roll for 1918 showed the family living at The Hollies, Belmont Road, Leatherhead. In 1937 Joseph lived at the Pumping Station, Gander Green Lane, Sutton, part of the Sutton and District Water Company site prior to its merger with East Surrey Water in the 1990's.

Humorous Postcard about Special Constables

ERNEST EVELYN MOY - Waterworks

Ernest was also named, in the *Surrey Advertiser* of the 12 July 1916, as one of the Epsom Rural Tribunal cases to be adjourned. He was born in 1877 in Skeyton, Norfolk, the son of a James and Rachael Moy. In 1881, Ernest lived with his widowed sixty-eight-year-old grandmother, who described herself of a farmer of twenty acres, and his parents in Lessingham. By 1901 twenty-four-year-old Ernest, an engine fitter, had married and lived with his new wife Sarah at Eton, in Buckinghamshire.

The 1911 Census gave his address as the Waterworks, Guildford Rd, Leatherhead where he and his wife Sarah, and their nine-year-old daughter Gwendoline who was born in Eton, resided. His occupation was recorded Waterworks Manager, Water Distribution. Kelly's Directories for 1911, 1913 and 1918 listed him as Engineer in charge of Leatherhead and District Water. The Electoral Roll for 1919 confirmed his address as the Waterworks. Ernest died in 1942 in Epsom Hospital.

REUBEN W HEATH- Chauffeur – 3 months' temporary exemption

The *Surrey Advertiser* of 11 November 1916 headlined, 'Military Representative's Chauffeur' stated, 'At a meeting of the Epson Rural Tribunal on Friday last week, Captain Pennethorne in the Chair, Mr Bernard Townsend, one of the military representatives, who lives in Fetcham, applied for the temporary exemption of his chauffeur and gardener, Reuben W Heath. He said that he had a large district to cover in the course of his work on behalf of the military, and if Heath had to be taken for the Army, he was afraid he would have to resign his position as military representative. He asked if the tribunal would grant him temporary exemption for three months. This was agreed to.'

In the 1911 Census Bernard Townsend was shown as a forty-five-year-old married solicitor with a seven-year-old daughter. They lived at 'Walden', in Bookham with a twenty-three-year-old cook and a twenty-four-year-old parlour maid.

G HILLYER - Yew Tree Cottage - Fetcham Appeal Refused.

The *Surrey Mirror* of 12 July 1918 stated the forty-four-year-old gardener at the Headmaster's House, Epsom Road, Leatherhead, had entered an appeal, which was supported by the Reverend. E A Downes. It was stated that in his spare time he assisted with farm work but the appeal was refused.

Hillyer, a carpenter labourer's son was born on 8 August 1873 in East Horsley. In 1911, thirty-eight-year-old George and his wife Ellen had been married for eleven years, but had no children. He was a bricklayer's labourer.

The Reverend Edmund Audley Downes was Headmaster in Holy Orders at St John's Foundation School for Sons of Poor Clergy of the Church of England in 1911. He was thirty-three years old and was born in Punjab, India. He and his wife Muriel from Kent, had a two-year-old daughter, and four servants, including a child's nurse, a cook, a parlour

maid, and a housemaid, although none of the servants were locals, coming from Dorset, Suffolk, Essex and Berkshire. It could be presumed that George Hillyer maintained the school grounds and possibly carried out handyman duties as well as helping out at a farm, although this is only supposition.

In 1939, fifty-year-old George worked as a gardener and he and his wife Ellen lived at 75 The Street, Cobham Road, Fetcham. He also lived at Yew tree Cottage in Fetcham until his death in February 1951.

Yew Tree Cottage, Fetcham

W H E RIVETT - River Lane - Fetcham Temporary Exemption

William Herbert Rivett was born in West Ham on 28 October 1898, a year after his father William Rivett Senior, a thirty-four-year-old School Master, had married Helen Lang of Home Farm, Fetcham at the Parish Church of St Mary's.

Marriage Register William Rivett and Helen Lang

Helen's father, William Lang had been born in Moray in Scotland and he and his wife moved to Fetcham in the 1880's bringing their whole farm stock, equipment and family from New Monkland to the east of Glasgow, to Home Farm by train – a familiar occurrence at this time. When William died in 1906, his two sons John and David, brothers of Helen, took over running Home Farm. In 1911 William Rivett's father was forty-eight and an Elementary School teacher and William Herbert himself was twelve. The family lived at 20 Clarendon Gardens, Ilford. William Herbert's name was to be published in the Surrey Advertiser of 12 June 1918. The article referred to a Surrey Appeal Tribunal meeting regarding 'twelve agricultural cases concerning men, who did not have the Agricultural Committee's certificate, and that under the present proclamation they would be automatically be called up.' 'The Chairman said perhaps the NSR would give them a reasonable amount of time so that substitutes could be got – Captain Courthorpe said his instructions were not to give time. The men should have joined up before'.

'The Chairman then suggested that the men should be left for three weeks so that the hay harvest could be got in and it was noted that in future all such cases would have to be subject to negotiations between the Agricultural Committee and the NSR.'

The tribunal referred to the person appealing for William's exemption was as his employer, D Lang of Home Farm, Fetcham. The case was recommended for temporary exemption to enable the man to be replaced. The Surrey Recruitment Registers show that William did indeed join the army on 30 June 1918 aged nineteen years and eight months. He was described as a farm student and enlisted with the Dragoon Guards, Service number C59059. He was a tall young man with a height of 6ft 1in and a 38 inch chest measurement and weighed 161 pounds. His address was Albany Crescent, Claygate.

In 1922 when David Lang moved from Home Farm to Claygate his sister Helen and her husband William Rivett Senior, and their son William Herbert moved to Home Farm. A year later in 1923 William Herbert married Madeline Murgatroyd.

THE APPEAL TRIBUNAL

The Military and Agriculture.

At the meeting of the Surrey Appeal Tribunal at Guildford on Saturday there were present: Sir Charles Walpole (chairman), General Sir Edmond Elles, Alderman A. C. Pain, Messrs. W. R. Skeet and H. Poulter, with the Clerk (Mr. M. A. Merriman), the National Service Representative (Capt. Courthope), and the Agricultural Representative (Mr. S. W. G. Tringham).

There were twelve agricultural cases, concerning men who did not have the Agricultural Committee's certificate, and it was mentioned that under the present Proclamation they would be automatically called up. — The Chairman said perhaps the N.S.R. would give them a reasonable amount of time so that substitutes could be got.—Capt. Courthope said his instructions were not to give time. The men should have joined up before. He would report what the tribunal said.—The Chairman suggested that the men should be left for three weeks, so that the hay harvest could be got in. In future all such cases would have to be the subject of negotiations between the Agricultural Committee and the N.S.R.

The men concerned were E. Tobbitt, Cranleigh, M. C Rapley, Thursley, W. H. Pyle, Ottershaw, Sidney Covey, Cranleigh, H. J. Heard, Shamley Green, F. Potter, Mytchett, E. Lucas, Abinger, W. Marshall, Puttenham, A. Botting, Coldharbour, J. Welsh, Holmwood, W. H. E. Rivett, Fetcham, and W. J. Edwards, Effingham.

The Surrey Mirror of 10 October 1924 carried am article on the Agricultural Association's Annual Match and Show at Priest Hill farm, Ewell, when 'heavy rain fell in the morning while the ploughing competitions were in progress, but the clouds rolled away about 2 o'clock and then the sun shone brightly. The entries showed a slight increase on last year, and the quality of the exhibits was up to the average, the ploughing took, being well carried out.' There were several sections in the competition: Ploughboys under 20, Ploughmen who have never won a premium, Ploughmen who have won a premium in a previous class and Champion Ploughmen. It appeared that J Williams representing William Rivett took third place in the penultimate section. William was to take second place for his Black Winter Oats. In the evening the annual dinner was held at the King's Head Hotel in Epsom.

CORN.

Yeoman milling wheat.—1, W. T. Curtis; 2, J. Wallace.

Milling wheat, other than yeoman.—1, J. Wallace; 2, Sir E. Mountain.

Malting Barley.—1, J. Wallace; 2, W. T. Curtis.

Black winter oats.—1, L. Thirlby; 2, W. H. Rivett.

White spring oats.—1, A. J. Brown; 2, S. M. Roberts.

Polesden Lacey challenge cup (given by the Hon. Mrs. Ronald Greville, Polesden Lacey.)—J. Wallace.

In the evening the annual dinner was held at the King's Head Hotel, Epsom, the chair being occupied by Sir A. R. Glyn (President.)

In 1926 William and Madeline were to have a son, William L Rivett, and three years later their daughter Evelyn was born. William's father William Rivett Senior died in 1936 aged seventy-nine and was buried in St Mary's churchyard and Home Farm ceased to be an actual farmhouse in 1938, although William's widowed mother Helen remained there until 1952 and was to celebrate her 100th birthday in 1969.

The Electoral Roll of 1933 showed William's wife Madeline was a qualified school teacher (like his own father) and ran a private school at Home Farm. An advertisement in 1938 referred to driving lessons being given by William and by 1939 and the start of World War 2 he was to serve at the Air Ministry at RAF Station, Hook. He was also for many years the Peoples Warden at the Church and a noted geologist and author of articles on the Geology of the Southeast and many of the fossil bones that he uncovered found their way to the Natural History Museum as the W H E Rivett Collection.

Madeline passed away in 1960 aged sixty-two but William enjoyed a long life like his 100 year old mother and was buried in St Mary's Churchyard on the 18 March 1998 aged 99.

Contextual Detail:

FindingNo	Level	Title	Date
DF100-DF199	Fonds	Department of Palaeontology	1739-2012
DF100	Series	Palaeontology Departmental Correspondence	1821-1979
DF100/185	File	Correspondence - individual files, Richter - Roberts	1890-1972

Level File

FindingNo DF100/185/17

Ref No DF PAL/100/185/17

Extent 19 pages

Title Rivett, W H E

Date 2 Nov 1948 - 20 Feb 1952

Description 19 letters, Leatherhead, Surrey, United Kingdom

Held By NHM Archives

Catalogue entry for William's collection, Natural History Museum.

CHAPTER FIVE

WAR HOSPITALS AND
VOLUNTARY AID DETACHMENTS

Some 90,000 volunteers worked at home and abroad during World War One supporting the armed services and caring for sick and wounded sailors and soldiers. The Red Cross had their own groups of volunteers called Voluntary Aid Detachments and members themselves came to be known simply as 'VADs'. They carried out a range of voluntary positions including nursing, transport duties, and the organisation of rest stations, working parties and auxiliary hospitals. At the outbreak of the war, many people were inspired to train to help the sick and wounded. Women were taught first aid, home nursing and hygiene by approved medical practitioners, and also took classes in cookery. Men were trained in first aid in-the-field and stretcher bearing. The VADs had to pass exams to receive their first aid and home nursing certificates.

In February 1915, the War Office proposed that volunteers could help at Military Royal Army Medical Corps (RAMC) hospitals. These had previously been staffed exclusively by army nurses and orderlies. The first request from military hospitals for these 'special service' VADs in England came early in 1915 and from France in May of the same year. These were quickly followed by demands from Malta and Egypt.

A 'general service' section of the VADs was established in September 1915. As men went off to fight VADs took their place, carrying out their roles such as dispensers, clerks, cooks and storekeepers. By 1919, 11,000 men had been released for active service and replaced by women. VADs were sent abroad during both world wars to countries such as France, Italy and Russia. Male detachments were frequently sent to France to work as transport officers or orderlies in hospitals. British Red Cross records indicate that the following Fetcham villagers served at the Red House Military Hospital in Leatherhead as members of the Voluntary Aid Detachment.

ALFRED THOMAS ALEXANDER, Stoke Road, Fetcham
Aged 17. Private 17th Surrey. October 1914–September 1915 Orderly Work 181 hours. Detraining wounded at Clandon Park Hospital. Killed in Action in France 3 September 1916 aged 19 serving with the Royal Army Medical Corps, 132nd Field Ambulance.

MRS JESSIE CALDWELL, Fetcham Rectory
January to September 1915 Office work.

REVEREND WILLIAM HENRY MCKENNAL CALDWELL, Fetcham Rectory
January to September 1917 Chaplain conducting weekly services and occasional visits. Subsequently volunteered to serve as an Army Chaplain France and Egypt.

WILLIAM DIVALL, Lower Lodge, Hawkshill
Private 17th Surrey. Orderly October 1914 to May 1916 part time 102 hours. Orderly duties. Detraining wounded Clandon Park Hospital. Died 1918 aged 48 and buried in St Mary's churchyard.

ALBERT ERNEST GRAVETT, The Bungalow, Surrey Gardens, Cobham

Previous address Fetcham Lodge, Fetcham. Aged 18. Private. Orderly duties. October 1914 to March 1915. Part time 151 hours. Detraining wounded Clandon Park Hospital. Later served as a Corporal Machine Gun Corps.

MISS THEODORA ANNE ELIZABETH GREEN, Ballands Hall Cottage, Fetcham

Full time. Enlistment 6 September 1915 Probationer. Termination June 1919. Staff Nurse. The member worked voluntarily for over 3 years – and only received pay on her appointment as Staff Nurse. Pay on Termination £20.

MRS OLIVE HANKEY, Fetcham Park House

November 1916 to 1917. Part time.

EDWARD WILLIAM JOHNSON, The Cottage, Fetcham

Private. October to December 1914. Orderly duties 15 hours' part time. 33 year old married Coachman/Groom born in Suffolk.

MISS MARGARET LANG, Home Farm, Fetcham

VAD Surrey 22 Nurse 28 October 1912 to February 1919. Part time 4,025 hours changing dressing and working on night duty. Her records show that she was awarded Proficiency Medal BRCB members medal and stripe and was mentioned in dispatches.

Local Red Cross working parties formed across the country with the co-operation of their surrounding villages. They organised the supply of hospital clothing including socks, shirts, blankets and belts for soldiers and made essential hospital equipment such as bandages, splints, swabs and clothing. Work depots were established in every major town to collate and despatch clothing from these working parties. Items were sent to Red Cross headquarters or directly to soldiers in auxiliary hospitals at home and abroad. Male detachments were almost entirely in charge of transporting sick and wounded soldiers from ambulance trains or ships to local hospitals. They also ferried patients between hospitals and were also frequently sent to France to work as ambulance drivers, often coming under fire as they transported men away from the Front.

On 27 February 1915, the Dorking and Leatherhead Advertiser published a report on the Men's Detachment of the 17th Surrey VAD which read:

'On Sunday last the members of the Men's Detachment of the 17th Surrey VAD accomplished a very smart performance. Information was received at the Red House shortly before three o'clock that assistance was required at Clandon to detrain some wounded soldiers who were expected to arrive there during the evening. In a little over an hour, fourteen men from Leatherhead, Ashtead and Fetcham and Mickleham, were ready to start from the Red House with five stretchers. In the unavoidable absence of the medical officer (Dr Dove), the men were in charge of the Quarter Master (Mr W T Lamming), and were accompanied by Section Leaders Palmer and Pinion.

The detachment made the journey to Clandon in motors, but as it happened their services were not required on Sunday as the wounded were not sent forward from the Base Hospital as soon as expected.'

On 28 December 1918, an article was published in the *Dorking and Leatherhead Advertiser* which read *'Twenty-four wounded soldiers spent Christmas at the Red Cross Hospital at the Red House, and no effort was spared to make their Christmas a most enjoyable one in every way. The wards were beautifully decorated with flags, evergreens and paper flowers, the patients having proved themselves adept at the making of clematis, wisteria, crimson ramblers and almond blossom, which were quite a feature of the decorations.*

The residents of the neighbourhood who have so splendidly supported the hospital through the years of the war were no less generous this Christmas, and seasonable gifts of all kinds were sent to the hospital for the patients. The Matron and the nursing staff also made their arrangements for the enjoyment of their patients and provided for each one a Christmas stocking with a seasonable gift in the morning and a bran tub in the afternoon. The Christmas dinner was a very substantial meal consisting of turkey, geese and ham, followed by Christmas pudding. Mrs Henderson and Mrs Still visited the hospital during the afternoon and distributed gifts to the patients, and in the evening, there were games of all kinds which were thoroughly enjoyed. On Thursday evening Mr Goddard's concert party visited the Red House and gave the inmates a very entertaining programme.'

The Red House Auxiliary Hospital, Bull Hill, Leatherhead

The hospital opened on 21 October 1914 in a property lent by Mr J W Burton. It had 20 beds and its first patients were wounded Belgian soldiers. The Hospital was under Eastern Command, affiliated to the Horton (County of London) War Hospital. Nursing staff consisted of a Matron and three Sisters, assisted by six members of the Surrey/22 Voluntary Aid Detachment (VAD) with the Surrey/17 VAD acting as orderlies. By the end of March 1915, it had thirty-three beds and was fully occupied. By 1916 this had been increased to thirty six beds and some 306 in-patients were treated. Many were severe cases who remained several months. The Hospital also treated out-patients (some eighty were seen in 1916), who were men on furlough (leave of absence), disabled soldiers or Army Service men doing farm work.

The Hospital did not have an operating theatre or X-ray Department, but provided general treatment, massage and electrical treatments-ionisation and catachresis (the introduction of drugs into the body by means of an electric current) and, later, wound irrigation. In 1917, the number of beds was increased to forty. The extra beds, bedding and blankets were all supplied to the Hospital by the local population.

An article dated 4 August 1917 appeared in the Dorking and Leatherhead Advertiser and read as follows:

'Leatherhead Division. The useful work being carried out by the Leatherhead Division is emphasised by the report of the Vice President Mrs John Henderson. The Division comprises of Leatherhead and the villages of Bookham, Effingham, Stoke D'Abernon, Oxshott, Ashtead, Mickleham and Fetcham. Mrs Henderson points out that there is one hospital in the Division, the Red House Auxiliary Hospital. Commandant, Dr Dove and Matron, Miss Bramwell. It was opened in October 1914 and continues to do excellent work'. 'The committee are most grateful to Mr J.W. Burton for his continued kindness in lending the Red House and to the hon. medical staff for their generosity in giving their time and skill to the patients. They also much appreciated the valuable help given by the Hon Treasurer, Mr C H Hawkins and thank the Hon Auditor Mr W Walter Read, FCA for his kindness in auditing the accounts. Mr Burley, late hon. Secretary to the hospital has taken up Red Cross work in France. The committee much regret his loss, but have been fortunate in securing Mr B M Waldock as his successor. Canon Hunter having resigned, the Reverend R B Maurice is kindly acting as Chaplain and holds a service every Sunday evening for the patients. Miss Joyce Coote has been posted to a British Hospital in France and the Misses Margery Cullen and Margaret Dixon to Military Hospitals at home. The sum collected in the Leatherhead Division on 'Our Day' amounted to £399 17s. 2d'. 'The Leatherhead Division still maintaining five beds in the Red Cross Hospital at Netley i.e. The Leatherhead Bed, per the Vice President, the Mickleham Bed per Mrs Lloyd, the Bookham and Effingham Bed, per Mrs Willock Pollen, the Randalls Bed, Mr and Mrs John Henderson and the Dalewood Bed, Captain and Mrs Widensham Fosbery.'

The Hospital closed in February 1919. During its operational lifetime, 698 in-patients had been treated. The low number reflects the seriousness of many of the cases (despite this, there were no deaths at the Hospital). In addition, 125 out-patients and 52 soldiers on the march had also received treatment. The house has now been demolished and

its site is now occupied by Fairmount House, an office development. The grounds of Red House have become an informal public garden, in the middle of the Leatherhead gyratory system. Source: Lost Hospitals of London

Site of the Red House Auxiliary Hospital, Leatherhead

The British Red Cross and Order of St John of Jerusalem

'At the outbreak of the First World War, the British Red Cross and the Order of St John of Jerusalem combined to form the Joint War Committee. They pooled their resources under the protection of the Red Cross emblem. As the Red Cross had secured buildings, equipment and staff, the organisation was able to set up temporary hospitals as soon as wounded men began to arrive from abroad.

The buildings varied widely, ranging from town halls and schools to large and small private houses, both in the country and in cities. The most suitable ones were established as auxiliary hospitals. Auxiliary hospitals were attached to central Military Hospitals, which looked after patients who remained under military control. There were over 3,000 auxiliary hospitals administered by Red Cross county directors. In many cases, women in the local neighbourhood volunteered on a part-time basis. The hospitals often needed to supplement voluntary work with paid roles, such as cooks. Local medics also volunteered, despite the extra strain that the medical profession was already under at that time. The patients at these hospitals were generally less seriously wounded than at other hospitals and they needed to convalesce. The servicemen preferred the auxiliary hospitals to military hospitals because they were not so strict, they were less crowded and the surroundings were homelier.

Apart from The Red House Auxiliary Hospital in Leatherhead there were by necessity other local auxiliary hospitals such as Heywood House in the Portsmouth Road, Cobham. The cigarette manufacturer, Walter Butler, offered the house to the War Office for use as an auxiliary military hospital. It opened in August 1915 as a Class B hospital affiliated to Horton (County of London) War Hospital. It had twenty-one beds and Mr Butler's wife, Mildred Mary, acted as Commandant. It was a convalescent hospital and by 1917 the number of beds had doubled to forty two. The Hospital became affiliated to Clandon Park Hospital, which had Lady Onslow as its Commandant. It is believed that the hospital closed at the end of 1918. Mrs Butler received an OBE in 1920 for her services during the war. The building is now the ACS Cobham International School. Other local hospitals included Clandon Park, Broom House, an Auxiliary to Clandon Park Hospital, West Horsley, Kirkstall and Dorking.

'Our Day'

'Our Day' was an annual fund raising event organised by the Red Cross instigated in 1915 and continuing throughout the war. The origin of the collection was considered to be 'Queen Alexander's Day', when the public showed its support for the Queen by buying flowers. 'Our Day' street collectors sold flags for a penny and silk ones for sixpence. Gifts for 'Our Day' were also received from abroad.

The local newspapers regularly published articles detailing the amount of money raised each year at these collections. In 1915 'the total collection for the Leatherhead Division was £309 7s.9d., with Leatherhead itself contributing £69 17s. 8d. Mrs Stanley Gordon Clark raised a total of £4 6s.1d. in Fetcham'. In 1916 Miss Mitford's Fetcham collection amounted to the sum of £8 11s.7d. and in 1917 Mrs Gordon Clark was to collect £6 3s.0d.

Surrey Advertiser 5 November 1917

"OUR DAY" RESULT.

The result of the recent collections in the Leatherhead Division on "Our Day" was highly satisfactory, the total amounting to £400 10s. 11d. The amounts collected in the eight parishes of the division were as follow: Ashtead (Mrs. Murray-Robertson), £67 10s. 2d.: Bookham and Effingham (Mrs. Willock-Pollen), £141 13s. 4d.; Fetcham (Mrs. C. S. Gordon Clark), £6 3s.; Leatherhead (Mr. C. Grantham), £57 19s. 11d.); Mickleham (Mrs. A. Gordon Pollock), £11 5s.; Oxshott (Mrs. Northcott), £102 4s. 6d.; Stoke D'Abernon (Mrs. Bristowe), £13 15s.

Red Cross working parties throughout the country organised the supply of bandages, splints, swabs and clothing for soldiers in hospital. Their work was co-ordinated by The Central Work Rooms set up in 1915 to train individuals to organise and instruct working parties and to promote uniformity by supplying standard patterns of hospital and surgical equipment in correct material, paper patterns, and books of instruction. Work depots were established in every major town to collate and despatch clothing including socks, shirts, belts and blankets from the working parties formed in the surrounding villages. Items were sent to the Red Cross headquarters or directly to soldiers in auxiliary hospitals at home or abroad. Surgical stores were also created to organise store supplies including sphagnum moss, chloroform and ether.

Fundraising was of vital importance throughout the First World War. Money and gifts-in-kind gathered through a variety of funds, collections and donations went towards services for soldiers both at home and abroad. By the end of the war, £21,885,035 had been raised and £20,058,355 spent on hospitals, medicine, clothing, grants and aftercare for the sick and wounded.

The Surrey Advertiser of 7 October 1916 carried the following article about the Supply Work Room at Fetcham Grove: 'WAR HOSPITAL SUPPLY WORK-ROOMS The first anniversary of the opening of these work room at Fetcham Grove was celebrated on Tuesday last week, when in response to an invitation from the committee, the lady patronesses, including Mrs S Gordon Clark, Mrs Henderson, Mrs MacAndrew, Mrs Still, Mrs Tritton and Mrs Willcock Pollen, kindly came to inspect the rooms and the work. Mrs Braithwaite, head of the Epsom Depot and the Vicar and Mrs Hobson were also present. There was a large attendance of workers, numbering nearly eighty. Mrs Willcock Pollen gave a short address and announced that the number of articles dispatched during the year was 8,610. With the exception of one or two consignments sent to the hospital for officers, 24 Park Street W, to the County of London War Hospital, Horton, Epsom everything had been sent to the Central Depot, 2 Cavendish Square, W, and had met with unqualified approval at headquarters. The money collected in Leatherhead, Ashtead, Fetcham and Mickleham, through the People's Penny Bandage collecting cards, amounted to £71 12s.0d. of which £67 had been sent to the central depot towards the purchase of materials, the remainder had been paid into the bank to meet expenses connected with the scheme. Tea was afterwards served.'

WAR WORKROOMS TO REMAIN OPEN
We are asked to state that in consequence of the urgent need for more and more bandages, swabs, etc., the War Hospital Supply workrooms at Fetcham Grove will not be closed as announced. Workers are earnestly asked to attend at least once or twice a week regularly. Gifts of old linen, old blankets, cretonne, chintz, felt cloth, etc., will be gratefully received. The working hours on Tuesdays, 11 to 1, and 2.15 to 6; Wednesdays and Thursdays, 2.15 to 6.

Surrey Advertiser of 27 January 1917

JESSIE ELIZABETH CALDWELL (nee oxley)

Jessie was born in Stoke Damerel, Devon in 1864 and married William Caldwell in Norwich in July 1896 when she was thirty-two years old. Their son Gavin was born the following year in Margate. During World War One, Jessie was initially to serve with the Voluntary Aid Detachment (VAD) whilst living at St Augustine's Vicarage before moving to Fetcham Rectory in 1916.

Surname	Caldwell
Christian Names	Jessie L. (Mr, Mrs. or Miss)
Permanent Address	St. Augustine's Vicarage Bristol. Fetcham Rectory Leatherhead.
Certificate No.	Age when engaged
Date of Engagement	Jan 1915 Rank Pay Col.
Date of Termination	Sept 1915 Rank Pay
Previous engagements under Joint War Committee, if any, and where	
Dept. for References	
Honours awarded	
Character	

VAD card for Jessie Caldwell giving address as St Augustine's Vicarage

Surname _Jessie Elsie Caldwell_ dec'd 9 AUG 1919

Christian Names _W._ (Mr., Mrs. or Miss)

Permanent Address _Fetcham Rectory_
Leatherhead

Date of Engagement _Sept 24th 1914_ **Rank** _Organizer_ **Pay** _Nil_

Date of Termination _Dec 16th 1914_ **Rank** **Pay** _Nil_

Particulars of Duties _Red X. Work Party at E. Hsey_

Whether whole or part time, and if latter No. of hours served _42_

Previous engagements under Joint War Committee, if any, and where _One of 6 Matrons_
at the Joint War Committee Red X. Clerkenwell. March
1915. August 1915. Acting Matron Holiday work at Passmore Edwards.

Honours awarded _Honorary Serving Sister Order of St John_
of Jerusalem.

PERIOD OF SERVICE. Etc. _Berkshire_

From _Sept 24th_ To _Dec 16th 1914_ { Commission or / Department or / County } _London_ / _Middlesex_

One of 6. Matrons under Dame Sarah Swift
at Clerkenwell choosing nurses for R.R.C
under Joint War Committee March 1915 –
August 31st 1915. One month July 1916
Acting Matron. The Passmore Edwards
Hospital "Auxiliary" Willesden. Middlesex
1917. Oct 2 weeks. Passmore Edwards Hos
Willesden) Auxiliary) Middlesex
Oct 22nd 1918 Nov 29th 5 weeks & 3 days
Passmore Edwards Hospital (auxiliary (Act Matron

The *VAD record card for Jessie Caldwell date stamped 9 August 1919*

Jessie was an 'Honorary Serving Sister Order of St John of Jerusalem'. Her service record stated that service started on 24 September and ended on 16 December 1914, and that she was 'one of 6 Matrons at the Joint War Committee Red Cross, Clerkenwell March 1915 to August 1915. Acting Matron Holiday Work at Passmore Edwards.' Rank on

Engagement: Organiser. Under Particulars of Duties the record reads 'Red Cross Work Party at E. Isey and under Additional Information: One of 6 Matrons under Dame Sarah Swift at Clerkenwell, choosing nurses for RRC under Joint War Committee March 1915 to 31 August 1915, one month. July 1916 Acting Matron, The Passmore Edwards Hospital, 'Auxiliary' Willesden, Middlesex. 1917 Oct. 2 weeks. Passmore Edwards Hos. Willesden (Auxiliary) Middlesex 22 Oct 1918 to 29 Nov 5 weeks & 3 days Passmore Edward Hospital (auxiliary) Act Matron.'

Passmore Edwards Hospital Willesden 1893

When the Joint War Committee took control of the VADs and trained nurses, these two departments were placed under the direction of Dame Sarah Swift, who had been Matron of St Guy's Hospital. From the outset of the war until November 1918, trained nurses were sent abroad at short notice under the banner of the Red Cross. Over 2,000 women offered their services in 1914, many declining a salary, and from this list individuals were despatched to areas of hostility including France, Belgium, Serbia and Gallipoli. From 1915, onwards they were joined by partially trained women from the VADs who were posted to undertake less technical duties. There are reports of unemployed trained nurses complaining that the wounded abroad were suffering from the lack of professional assistance whilst many women were simply waiting at home, keen to offer their services. Yet the War Office and the Joint Committee considered that with an escalating number of wounded servicemen being sent home, fewer nurses were required abroad. This resulted in an increase in the ranks of paid nurses being employed in hospitals at home'.

In February 1918 Jessie's husband William was one of the survivors on board the ship 'Aragon' when it was attacked by enemy action and sank and their only son Gavin was to be killed in action in October 1918. Jessie died in October 1936 aged seventy-two. See 'Rectors of St Mary's-Rev. William Henry McKennal Caldwell' and 'Candlesticks and a Gold Watch'

Life in a military hospital

An article from the *Dorking and Leatherhead Advertiser* dated 8 May 1915 reported Pte W Day of the RAMC (Royal Army Medical Corps) writing to Mr and Mrs Budd of Fetcham and gives an interesting account of the work of a general war hospital at home. He says: *'We had about 120 wounded arrive this week, most of them coming from Hill 60. I will try to describe as near as I possibly can the routine in a military hospital. We receive a telegram informing us of the number of wounded coming, and later another message announcing the time of arrival.*

The hospital orderlies are divided into two companies – one for the railway station to unload the train and put the men on the ambulances, the other to unload at the hospital and take the men to the different wards as directed by the

medical officer in charge of the hospital. There is no elaborate show about the interior of the Red Cross train, it is all for comfort. The beds in the coaches are practically the same as on board ship, one over the other on both sides, with plenty of room between for the orderlies to move about. Most of the trains have a special car fitted up with a kitchen, operating theatre and everything else that is likely to be wanted. Those patients that are unable to speak have a little tab, like a luggage label, tied on their coats, describing their wounds. In the hospital the patient is undressed, and if he is unable to walk he is given a blanket bath, and if he can walk he is taken to the bath room attached to each ward. If the man has been wounded by a rifle bullet or shrapnel an X ray photograph is taken. When the man is fit for the operation, which is usually two or three days after his arrival, the sister in charge of the ward ascertains if he is willing to undergo it. The patients in a military hospital are as a rule much more cheerful than in a civil hospital. Of course, Tommy is never happy unless he has a cigarette to smoke, and any patient well enough to go out in the grounds can smoke all day if he wishes.'

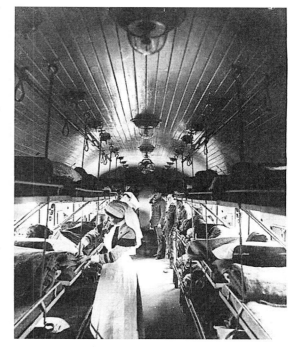

Interior of a British Ambulance Train

Silver War Badge

Many thousands of the servicemen and women who were hospitalised during the World War One were unable to return to active service because of injuries sustained or illness. Men of military age who were not obviously in the services were sometimes presented by civilians with white feathers — a symbol of cowardice — believing them to be shirking their patriotic duty.

In September 1916, King George V authorized the Silver War Badge (SWB) to honour all military personnel who had served at home or overseas since 4 August 1914 and who had been discharged because of wounds or illness. It was a small, circular badge made of sterling silver, which bore the king's initials, a crown, and the inscriptions '*For King and Empire*' and '*Services Rendered*' and served to show that the wearer had served his country. Almost fifty percent of the two million military personnel discharged from the armed forces during the war for illness or injury, including those who had served from anywhere in the British Empire, and those who left before it was instituted in 1916, applied to wear the SWB.

When researching an individual's military service in World War One and no service records can be found, the Silver War Badge records may be the only remaining evidence of their involvement. The Records include rank, regimental number, unit, dates of enlistment and discharge, and reason for discharge.

ROSE KATHLEEN STOVELL - Women's Army Auxiliary Corps (WAAC)

Rose was born on 15 October 1899 in Fetcham and baptised under the name of Katharine Rose on 26 November 1899 in St Mary's Church. Her Parents were George Stovell and Grace Annie (nee Diment). The 1901 Census showed Rose living with her parents at Fetcham Common, where her father worked as a stockman. Her younger brother George was born in 1902. By 1911 the family were living in The Street, Fetcham and Rose and George attended Fetcham Village School. According to the School Log Book, after being unsuccessful in July 1912, she successful passed her Labour Examination in July 1913 and left school. Her brother George left three years later aged fourteen.

Rose's mother Grace was one of ten children, all born in Fetcham and her five brothers all served during World War One. Sadly, two of them were to lose their lives. This may have had an influence on Rose's enlistment in the WAAC when she was eighteen year's old.

In 1917, as the war drained Britain's manpower, an official force of women soldiers embarked for France in uniform for the first time. The WAAC was formed to free up valuable and experienced soldiers from the rear areas for front line service. As part of the mobilisation of the whole country this milestone in the push for equal rights formed the basis for women's service in the British Army to this day. By 1918, nearly 40,000 women had enrolled. Of these, some 7,000 served on the Western Front, the rest back in the United Kingdom. Their overall conduct led to Queen Mary becoming the patron of the Corps. On 9 April 1918, it was renamed Queen Mary's Army Auxiliary Corps (QMAAC) in honour of their bravery'. Service records for the QWAAC indicate Rose's enrolment station was at 28 Warwick Square, London. Her service number 38704. She was allocated to Mobile Branch (category B) as a waitress.

On the application to the Women's Royal Auxiliary Corp, in April 1918, Rose gave her residence as c/o Lady Duckham, Highfields, Ashtead her referee was W J Weller, Esq Town Councillor, of 3 Popular Road, Leatherhead. Mr Weller responded that *'he had known Rose two years and upwards as a domestic servant and considered her steady, reliable and industrious, a fit person to be trusted with confidential documents'*. Lady Duckham, of Highfields, Ashtead vouched that she had known Rose for two years and gave a similar character reference. A third reference came from Mary Munro, the matron of Leatherhead Cottage Hospital who stated that Rose had been house parlour maid there from December 1914 to May 1916. *'She had waited at table and frequently on patients when they were busy and she was very quick and capable'*. A Medical History Form showed that she was medically examined at 2 Hyde Park Street on 30 April 1919. She gave her birthplace as Fetcham, Surrey and her religion as Wesleyan. She was five feet two and a half inches tall and weighed 116lbs. Her chest measurement was thirty-one and a half inches and it was stated that she had good physical development. Four vaccination marks on her left arm were also noted. Her age on enlistment was eighteen years and ten months and her occupation

'Waitress'. A 'Requisition for Free Clothing' form dated 13 June 1919 from Station Connaught Club, W2 (QMAAC Headquarters) was submitted and Rose was issued with the following items of uniform: Coat frock, one pair of shoes, two stockings, four overalls, four caps, and three collars for which she signed for as being in good condition on 17 September 1919.

Women's Auxiliary Army Corps waitresses, c1917

A further form 'Admission to Hospital or Sick List' showed that she was hospitalised three times during her service, the first occasion on the 18 June 1918 when she spent five days in the QMAAC Sick Hostel in Holland Park suffering from Influenza. She was again admitted in February 1919 spending eight days in hospital again with Influenza. The Spanish Influenza epidemic of 1918-19 killed millions across the world, and Lia Parfit a member of the QWAAC in 1917 was to later recall in her memoirs *'the Spanish Flu epidemic swept over the whole command like a whirlwind leaving many vacant places in our ranks... Every hospital was filled beyond capacity, and as soon as we were able to stand on our feet we were discharged for light duty.'* Rose's final hospitalisation was in July 1919 when she spent nine days in hospital with Tonsillitis.

With the end of the war, the QMAAC were no longer of use in an army being cut down in size to peacetime levels. On 27 Sept 1921, the QMAAC was formally disbanded. The Corps maintained a very healthy Old Comrades Association and these links remained throughout the period between the two World Wars. Some women organised themselves into an 'Emergency Service' which could be mobilised if required. On 11 February 1922 Rose married twenty three year old Ernest George Robbins Winter, a plate layer at St Mary's Church, Fetcham.

CHAPTER SIX

FETCHAM WAR MEMORIAL

In 1919, at the end of World War 1, it was proposed that a public Meeting be held in Fetcham to consider the matter of a War Memorial and a Parish Celebration of Peace. The Fetcham Memorial, like so many others around the country, was funded by local contributions, to commemorate the war dead.

The Epsom Rural District Council Minutes Reports, Highway and General Purposes Committee Minutes of 29 October 1919 read as follow: 'Present amongst the others Reverend W H Mc Caldwell. The surveyor reported that Mr Woods of the Salt Box applied on behalf of several residents, consent to the erection of a Memorial Cross at the junction of River Lane and Stoke Road and that the Memorial would be placed on the metalled highway. Resolved that Mr Woods be informed that the council had no power to grant permission for the erection of the memorial but they would raise no objection.'

The Memorial Cross of stone was originally erected at the junction of River Lane and Stoke Road, opposite to The Reading Rooms in 1920, the designer unknown. It consists of three stepped octagonal bases surmounted by plinth, tapering shaft and Latin Cross. It stands approximately 4 metres high. Twelve names of Fetcham men were inscribed on the stonework, including two sets of brothers, Charles and Thomas Belton, who died within three months of each other and Albert and John Diment.

Pte. 65929 Alfred Alexander	Royal Army Medical Corps.
Pte. 406670 Charles Henry Belton	Canadian Infantry (Western Ontario Regiment)
Gnr. L/47104 Thomas Ernest Belton	Royal Field Artillery
Lt. Gavin R M Caldwell	2nd.Bn.Coldstream Guards
Pte. G/2317 Albert Diment	The Queens (Royal West Surrey)
Pte. 26457 John H Diment	Labour Corps
Rfm.4574 Ernest O R Hinder	Queens Westminster's
Pte. 8253 Frederick C Johnson	East Surrey Regiment
Lance Corporal 24895 Alfred W Medd	Queens (Royal West Surrey
Gnr. Thomas	
Capt. Leslie Woods	Royal Field Artillery
Cpl. 12582 E Worsfold	Coldstream Guard

Original site of the War Memorial at the junction of Stoke Road and River Lane.

Twenty-two more casualties were added and in 1948 it was decided to re-site the Cross. Eight tenders were sought for its re-siting and in 1949 Franks Harris Bros Ltd of Sutton tender of £1,649 19s. 6d. was accepted. The Memorial was subsequently moved to the Garden of Remembrance, off The Ridgeway, where it now stands and has been added to Historic England's List of Buildings of Special Architectural or Historic Interest, Grade II.

Inscription 'In memory of the men of Fetcham who gave their lives for King and Country in the Great Wars 1914- 1919 / 1939–1945'.

Present site in Garden of Remembrance

CHAPTER SEVEN

INDIVIDUAL STORIES

JOHN WILLIAM ALDRIDGE

John was born on 26 June 1887 in Petersham, Surrey. He was the son of Lucy and John Arnold Aldridge, a Market Gardener and had an elder sister Margaret and a younger brother Raymond. The family moved to West Horsley sometime before 1901 and in the census of that year his father was described as a Farmer. By 1911 John had moved to Fetcham and was lodging with Thomas Grubb and his family. Both Thomas and John were Game Keepers. The

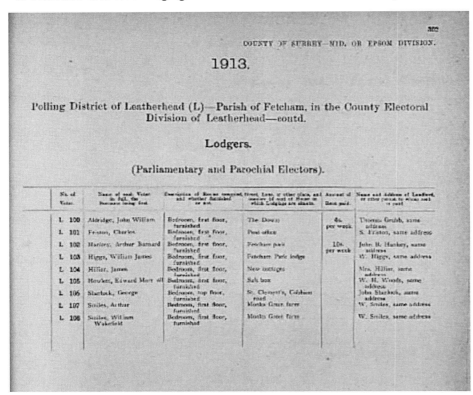

1913 Parliamentary and Parochial Electoral Register showed John as a Lodger with Thomas Grubb and paying 4s.0d a week rent for a furnished bedroom on the first floor.

In April 1913 twenty five year old John married Edith Matthews in Ockham Parish Church. Three years later in July 1916 he enlisted in the Middlesex Regiment as a Private, Regimental Number 6431. He was described as five feet, eight inches tall, weighting 133 lbs and with a chest measurement of 35 inches and of good physical development. His name listed on the list of individuals entitled to the Silver War Badge indicating that sadly he was wounded and was discharged on 8 November 1918.

1913 Parliamentary and Parochial Electors John William Aldridge

Silver War Badge entry John William Aldridge

ALFRED ALEXANDER

Alfred was the son of Thomas Alexander and Harriett Diment, and was baptised on 2 May 1897 in St Mary's Church, Fetcham. As well as his twin brother Charles, he had younger brothers Frederick, George, Frank and Ernest and two sisters, Ethel and Dorothy. The family lived in River Lane and Alfred attended the local village school, according to the Fetcham School Log Book, and left in 1911.

As a young man and in the early stages of World War One Red Cross records showed Alfred worked part time as an orderly at The Red House Auxiliary Hospital in Leatherhead from October 1914 until September 1915, completing a total of 181 hours of work.

Alfred Alexander VAD Card

When he was nineteen years old, he joined the Royal Army Medical Corps (132nd Field Ambulance), Service Number 65929, and gave his parents address as Tea Tree Cottage, Fetcham. Sadly, he was to lose his life on 3 September 1916 and is remembered at the Knightsbridge Cemetery, Mesnil Martinsart, France.

Martinsart was close to the Allied front line until September 1916, and again from March to August 1918. Martinsart British Cemetery was begun at the end of June 1916, when fourteen men of the 13th Royal Irish Rifles, killed by a shell, were buried in what is now Plot 1, Row A. It was used as a front-line cemetery until October 1916 and

again in September 1918, when bodies were brought in from the battlefields for burial by V Corps. After the Armistice, the cemetery was enlarged when more graves were brought in from the area north, east and south of the village.

'An Attack: Reserves Moving Up' The photograph was taken during the 1916 Somme offensive and among the combat troops going forward is a regimental stretcher bearer.

The 132nd Field Ambulance, Royal Army Medical Corps served with 39th Division. The Division was formed in the Winchester area in early August 1915. On 30 June 1916, they were in action in an attack near Richebourg l'Avoue with the Sussex battalions suffering heavy casualties.   They were in action during the Battles of the Somme, including the fighting on the Ancre, The Battle of Thiepval Ridge.

A newspaper article dated 16 September 1916 reported Alfred's death:

'On Tuesday, last Mr. and Mrs. Alexander of Teatree Cottages, Fetcham, received intimation that one of their twin sons, Pte. Alfred Thomas Alexander of the AMC had made the great sacrifice.

In a letter to Mrs. Alexander dated 7 September, Pte. A Axtell wrote 'I am very sorry to tell you Alfred died at one last Sunday. He was quite cheerful to the last. He spoke of you in his last words, and asked me to write to you. He was laid to rest on the Monday. We all sympathise with you in the loss of your son'. On Wednesday evening the following letter dated Sept 10th was received from Pte. M H King: 'Being one your son's chums, I think it is my duty to write to you and express my deep regret and sincere sympathy in this your time of trouble. Alec and I were in hut together for over three months. He was liked by all with the ambulance. He was a ready worker. He met his death like a hero. While bringing in a wounded comrade down the trenches a shell burst over them and Alec was killed. There was very little hope for him and he passed peacefully away in a few minutes.'

Pte. Alfred Alexander, who was 19 years of age, was for some time a popular member of the Leatherhead VAD and gained his certificate for proficiency. As soon as he was able, he joined the AMC and after a brief training at Fleet went out to France in January last. At the time, he enlisted he was in the employ of Capt. Henry Keswick, MP, at Tyrrells Wood, Leatherhead. Mr. and Mrs. Alexander's other twin son, Pte. Charles Alexander, who is in the Machine Gun Section, was wounded in France about three months ago and at the present time is in hospital at Grantham.'

CHARLES JAMES ALEXANDER

Charles Alexander was Alfred's twin brother but the twins were not christened at the same time, Charles was privately baptised on 14 April 1897 and Alfred later, on 2 May. Both attended the local school and left in April 1911. As a seventeen-year-old carpenter, Charles enlisted on the 28 March 1914 in Leatherhead, into the 5th battalion of the East Surrey Regiment, Regimental Number 1806. He was described as being five foot two inches tall, and inch or so shorter than Alfred, but with good physical development.

The following year on 11 May 1915, eighteen years old Charles joined up but unlike his twin Alfred who joined the Royal Army Medical Corps, Charles was to serve with the Queen's Royal West Surrey Regiment, Regimental Number 1102. He later served with the newly formed Machine Gun Corps, (MGC) Regimental Number15047, reaching the rank of Corporal.

Surrey Regimental Rolls, 1914-1947 for Charles James Alexander Queen's Royal West Surrey 1919-1929 Enlistment Register, Odd Numbers

55

On 2 September 1915, a definite proposal was made to the War Office for the formation of a single specialist Machine Gun Company per infantry brigade, by withdrawing the guns and gun teams from the battalions. They would be replaced at battalion level by the light Lewis machine guns and thus the firepower of each brigade would be substantially increased. The Machine Gun Corps was created by Royal Warrant on 14 October followed by an Army Order on 22 October 1915. The companies formed in each brigade would transfer to the new Corps. The MGC would eventually consist of infantry Machine Gun Companies, cavalry Machine Gun Squadrons and Motor Machine Gun Batteries.

The Earl and Countess Brownlow offered the parkland of their home at Belton House, near Grantham, Lincolnshire to the Army for the formation of the Machine Gun Corps and some 170,500 officers and men served in the MGC, the men being trained to use Vickers machine guns and sent all over the world. At any one time between 1915 and 1922 there were thousands of men on the camp.

The pace of reorganisation depended largely on the rate of supply of the Lewis guns but it was completed before the Battle of the Somme in 1916. A Base Depot for the Corps was established at Camiers.

Machine Gun Corps poster

Machine Gun Corp badge

The huts at Belton

Members of the MGC

Belton House.

We're the Corps born yesterday
We're the Corps that's come to stay
(and there'll be the devil to pay)
We're the MGC

We know no fear or favour
We're not given to palaver
We're never known to waver
We're the MGC

We're in the van of the attack
And, when things are looking black
We're in the rear to hold them back
We're the MGC

You should hear the bullets zip
When our guns are on the rip
And we smite them thigh and hip
We're the MGC

We are always on the spot
Where'er the fight is hot
Till all the team is shot
We're the MGC

We're the Corps born yesterday
We're the Corps that's come to stay
We're the Corps that earns our pay
We're the MGC

F L Shaw 1915

At the end of hostilities, the MGC was again re-organised in a smaller form as many of its soldiers returned to civilian life. By 1920 the headquarters in Belton Park was closed.

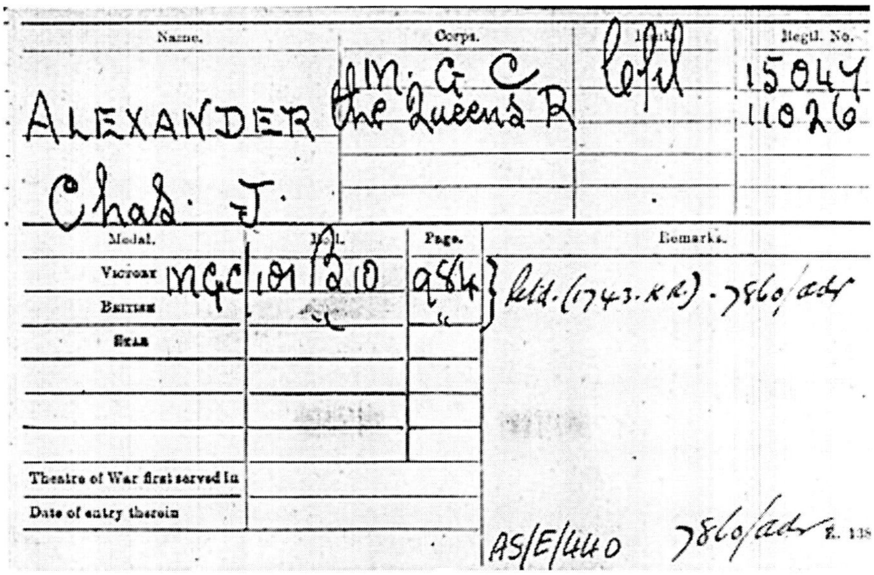

Name.	Corps.	Rank.	Regtl. No.
ALEXANDER Chas. J.	M.G.C. / The Queen's R	Cpl	15047 / 11026

Medal.	Roll.	Page.	Remarks.
Victory	MGC 101 B10	984	} Rtd. (1743 K.R.) 7860/adr
British			
Star			
Theatre of War first served in			
Date of entry therein			AS/E/440 7860/adr

Charles's Medal Card showed that he served in the 101st battalion of the Machine Gun Corps, and referred to his medal being 'Returned (1743 Kings Regulations). This may have been because there was an error in the inscription, in which case the medals would have to be returned to the Medals Office. Another reason for return was if the individual had moved house and the parcel was not deliverable, although it is understood that some men simply did not want a medal.

Charles Alexander's medal card

The 101st Brigade 34th Division were in action during the Battles of the Somme, including the capture of Scots and Sausage Redoubts, The Battles of Bazentin Ridge and Pozieres Ridge.

The newspaper article dated 16 September 1916 reported Charles twin brother Alfred's death and also referred to Charles as having been wounded in France about three months earlier and being in hospital at Grantham.

Grantham Red Cross Hospital   *Red Cross Hospital, Grantham Barracks, Sandon Road. 1914*

On 3 November 1917 Charles married Nellie Ada Burridge at St George's Church, Old Brentford. She was twenty-three years old, two years older that Charles whose occupation was given as Soldier.

The 1920 Electoral Roll showed Charles living at Cobham Road with his parents, Thomas and Harriett and brother Frederick, but by 1926 the couple had moved to Crabtree Lane, Great Bookham.

REDVERS VICTOR ANSELL

Redvers was born on 3 March and was the son of Amelia (nee Tidy) and her gardener husband Mark. He was baptised at St Mary's Church, Fetcham on the 6 May 1900. The family lived at Hawks Hill Lodge and Redvers attended the Village School winning school prizes in both 1911 and 1912.

28 July   Completed the 3rd Term's examination. Weekly Average 49.2 = 88%. 90 on books. James and Eva Whiten have left.
Donald Wild is leaving, having gained a County Scholarship, for Dorking High School. Cecil Knowles, aged 13, Std. VI is leaving for the same school. The following is a list of prize winners in the Term examination.
Std. VI George Lambert, 82 marks Violet Shuffill 83.
Std. V R. Ansell 89. Marjorie Portsmouth 90
" IV. Eric Wild 73. Muriel Burfoot 83.
Total marks 90.

School Log Book 1911

58

Redvers's name was recorded in several local newspapers of the time, the first in 1909 when the Leatherhead and District Fanciers' Society held their annual members show at Victoria Hall and Redvers was to come first in the children's poultry section. According to the Surrey Mirror of 8 August 1911 the annual show at Eastwick Park 'was favoured with fine weather and was again a brilliant success with entries totalling over five hundred'. Redvers was amongst those children mentioned – coming fourth for his bouquet of wild flowers and second to Henry Gravett for his collection of queen wasps. The article continued with a report of an 'early evening programme of athletic sports' and 'a capital lot of sideshows provided for the enjoyment of visitors'.

Surrey Mirror 8 August 1911

SCHOOL CHILDREN.

Bouquet of wild flowers: 1 Alfred Atkin, 2 May Stemp, 3 Kate Amey, 4 Redvers Ansell; Bunch of sweet peas: 1 Alfred Atkins, 2 Geo. Cook, 3 Mildred Gravatt, 4 Hilda Gravatt, 5 Lillie Watkinson; Collection of queen wasps: 1 Henry Gravatt, 2 Redvers Ansell.

The Dorking and Leatherhead Advertiser of 13 July 1912 listed the County Junior Scholarships being offered, 100 Class A and 20 Class B. One hundred and fifty-three children were candidates in Class B, of which thirty-three qualified for the final examination. The final oral examinations were held at County Hall, Kingston with Redvers being one of the successful children in Class B.

Redvers V. Ansell, Fetcham C.E.	426	74
Charles J. Dale, Shere	425	76
Ronald H. Shipley, Cobham C.E.	419	82
Katherine L. Winton. Coulsdon,		

Extract Dorking and Leatherhead Advertiser July 1912

Redvers's name was recorded in the Fetcham School Log Book of 2 September as having left to attend High School. His father Mark passed away three years later in July 1915 at the age of forty-seven. On leaving school Redvers took up employment as a Commercial Clerk.

School photo – Redvers is possibly the middle boy in the middle row. Fetcham 1910.

Like Henry Cooper, another young man from Fetcham, Redvers joined a Young Soldiers Battalion when he had just turned eighteen. On 2 April 1918, he enlisted with the Royal Sussex Regiment (53rd YSB), part of the 23rd Reserve Brigade and would have undertaken basic training in Aldershot. He was five feet seven inches tall at the time and weighed 128 lbs with a 34-inch chest measurement.

Redvers Ansell aged eighteen.

In 1926 he was living at The Bungalow, Kings Mead, Leatherhead and wed Louie May Alexandra Bevand in Leatherhead Parish Church on 10 July 1926. On his marriage certificate he described himself under Rank or Profession as a 'Manager'. His bride's home address was given as Red House Lodge, Leatherhead. The couple lived at The Bungalow until 1933 before moving to 25 Kingscroft Road, Leatherhead and celebrated their Golden Wedding in 1976. Two years later Redvers passed away.

R V Ansell, taken 12 Jan 1919 at Blackdown Camp. Photo is credited to photographer A Warren, The Cresent, Leatherhead Blackdown Camp at Pirbright Surrey.

Wedding photograph 10 July 1926 Redvers Ansell and Louie May Alexandra

ARTHUR LEWIS BEARSBY Three-year-old Arthur appeared in the 1881 Census. His father Eli Bearsby was a Gamekeeper and the family lived at Court Lodge, Keepers Cottage, Lamberhurst. Some twenty years on the 1901 Census showed twenty-three-year-old Arthur had followed his father's occupation as a Gamekeeper, and was a Boarder at Willoughby Cottages, Farleigh. In January 1907 he married in Paddington, and four years later Gamekeeper Arthur and his wife Katherine who came from Chichester, were both in their thirties, and living at The Kennels, Fetcham. The couple had a two-year-old son, Arthur Frederick who had been baptised in St Mary's Church, Fetcham on 9 August 1908.

Arthur was to serve with 1st Battalion the Queen's (Royal West Surrey) Regiment as Private G/37027. Their records indicate that he was taken a prisoner of war.

Surname	Initials	First names	Rank	Battalion	Regimental number	Town	County	Transcriber's notes	Page	Side	Reference
Bartram	F	Frederick William	Pte	2nd	22397	Bedford	Bedfordshire	Arrived Holland 14 January 1918	17	Left	QRWS/1/5/1
Baseley	F	Frank	Pte	7th	8763	Kilburn	London	Died February 12 1917 at Hambling. Buried at Niederwehren Cemetery	16	Right	QRWS/1/5/1
Bass	H C	Henry C	Pte	11th	207041	Ipswich	Suffolk	Also 265491 Suffolk Regiment	24	Left	QRWS/1/5/1
Bassett	J	Joseph Ernest	Pte	8th	3061	Rusthall	Kent		15	Left	QRWS/1/5/1
Basten	A	Adolphe	Sgt	7th	2581	Fulham	London		25	Left	QRWS/1/5/1
Batchelor	L	Lewis	LCpl	24th	68898	Gillingham	Kent	London Regiment	25	Left	QRWS/1/5/1
Bateman	G	George	LCpl	1st	8195	Sundridge	Kent	Sister living in Kentish Town	10	Left	QRWS/1/5/1
Bateman	W A	William A	Pte	8th	12881	Enfield	Middlesex		21	Left	QRWS/1/5/1
Bath	G L	George Leonard	Pte	1st	9451	Battersea	London		18	Right	QRWS/1/5/1
Battern	W	William	Pte	7th	68941	Watlington	Oxfordshire		25	Left	QRWS/1/5/1
Baughn	J	John	Cpl	1st	8888	Brockley	London		19	Left	QRWS/1/5/1
Baverstock	E	Ernest	Sgt	1st	6120	West Clandon	Surrey	Arrived Holland 16 May 1918	15	Right	QRWS/1/5/1
Bawn	E G	Edward G	Pte	11th	243101	Frenchay	Gloucestershire		25	Left	QRWS/1/5/1
Baxter	A	Arthur	Pte	11th	25683	Idle	Yorkshire		23	Left	QRWS/1/5/1
Baxter	J W	James W	Pte	7th	21136	Diss	Norfolk		16	Right	QRWS/1/5/1
Bayley	C S	Cecil	Pte	8th	201537	Croydon	Surrey		19	Right	QRWS/1/5/1
Baylis	H	Henry	Pte	10th	207917			Missing. Formerly 2873 1/1st Surrey Yeomanry	24	Right	QRWS/1/5/1
Beadle	F C	Frederick C	Pte	6th	200189	Croydon	Surrey	Formerly T/1388 QRWS	24	Right	QRWS/1/5/1
Beardsby	A L	Arthur Lewis	Pte	1st	37027	Fetcham	Surrey		18	Right	QRWS/1/5/1
Beckett	W	William	Pte	1st	5185	Clerkenwell	London		18	Left	QRWS/1/5/1

After the war, Arthur returned to his home in Fetcham and can be found in the 1922 Electoral Rolls living at the Old Kennels. His death was recorded in the September quarter of 1953 in Surrey.

THE BELTON FAMILY

George Belton was born in Fetcham in 1858 and married Jane Sayers in 1880. Although she was born in Effingham by the 1871 census she was living with her family in Fetcham. The couple lived in Cobham Road in Fetcham and George worked as an agricultural labourer. Their eldest son George William was born in 1881, and two years later a daughter Edith was born. The family grew as Sarah was born in 1885, Emily in 1886, Charles 1889 and Thomas Ernie (often referred to as Ernest) who was born in 1891. In 1901, the family lived at River Lane and George described his occupation as a carpenter on a farm. Son George was a farm labourer and Emily was employed as a domestic servant. Their three sons went to war – but only one returned.

George William married Florence Matthews in November 1907 at St Peter's Church in Croydon and joined the army in November 1915 at the age of thirty-four. He was described as five feet nine inches tall and weighed 141 lbs and was posted to the 3rd Battalion of the East Surrey Regiment.

Charles became a gardener and in 1911 was living in Sutton with his Aunt and Uncle, Emma and William Sayers and their son Harry. Uncle William was also a gardener and Harry worked as a chauffeur. Charles emigrated to Canada to start a new life, probably early in 1914 and as a Canadian National enlisted with the 1st Battalion Canadian Infantry (Western Ontario Regiment) on 20 April 1915. Their records show he stood six feet one inches, a tall man for the time.

Canadian Recruitment Posters

The 1st Canadian Infantry Battalion was a Battalion of the Canadian Expeditionary Force seeing action at Ypres and along the Western Front. He was posted 'Missing Presumed Killed' on 13 June 1916 aged twenty-seven, presumably during the Battle of Mount Sorrel which took place from the 2-13 June. He is remembered at the Menin Gate Memorial to the Missing, a war memorial in Ypres, Belgium, dedicated to the British and Commonwealth soldiers who were killed in the Ypres Salient of World War I and whose graves are unknown. The memorial is located at the eastern exit of the town and marks the starting point for one of the main roads out of the town that led Allied soldiers to the front line. Remembered here amongst others are 40,244 soldiers from the United Kingdom, 6,983 Canadians and 6,198 Australians.

Canadian Infantry (Western Ontario Regiment) cap badge

Panoramic view of the 1st Canadian Infantry Battalion at Valcartier, Qc. Most of the soldiers in this photograph would likely have been killed or wounded by the end of the war due to the terrible casualty rates suffered by front-line infantry battalions.

Twenty-seven-year-old Emily Belton was to marry Sidney Albert Vass at St Mary's in Fetcham in April 1913. He was from Aldershot and was employed as a groom.

Thomas Ernie was the couple's youngest son and sadly just three months after his brother's death Charles was to lose his life in the conflict. He left Fetcham Village School in 1905 as a fourteen-year-old and with the outbreak of war enlisted in Wimbledon and served with the Royal Field Artillery Regimental Number L/47104 with the rank of Acting Bombardier. He was killed in action on the 26 September 1916 in the Battle of Morval when Combles, Morval, Lesbœufs and Gueudecourt were captured and many casualties inflicted on the Germans. The War Diary for the unit dated 26 September recorded 'We take Lesboeufs and Morval and join the French in Combles. Casualties 47104 Belton, Killed, 41314 Sutcliffe, 45216 Hitchcock and 47138 Beckley Wounded'.

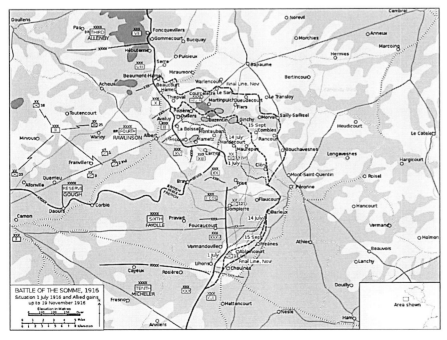

Royal Artillery War Diary listing the death of Thomas Ernest Belton 26 September 1916.

Combles was attacked by the British and French on 25 September, during the Battle of Morval after several delays due to rain and poor visibility. Brigades from the 56th and 5th Divisions in the north, wheeled to the right to form a south-facing flank above Combles, as the French 2nd Division attacked from the south. The British attack swiftly established the defensive flank and patrols began to probe southwards. German resistance against the French attack close to the village, particularly with machine-gun fire, held back the advance but further east,

Map Anglo-French attack at Combles, Somme, 25 September 1916

the French captured Rancourt in the afternoon and closed up to Frégicourt. Prisoners taken by the British and French, revealed a retirement from the village was intended during the night. A constant Allied artillery barrage was maintained on the exits. Infantry patrols probed forward and the British and French forces met at several points in and east of the village, in the early hours of 26 September. A huge amount of equipment, ammunition and engineering stores were captured in the village and on 27 September, the inter-army boundary was moved north to Morval, to assist French attacks towards Sailly-Saillisel.

Combles 1916

BDR. T. E. BELTON, R.F.A.
Killed in Action.

Mr. and Mrs. Belton, of River-lane, Fetcham, have received news of the death of their son, Bdr. T. E. Belton, killed in action on September 26th. He was 25 years of age, a keen and zealous soldier, and much respected by the officers and men of the Battery, who have sent to the bereaved parents their sincere condolences. Bdr. Belton's loss is particularly felt by the Battery, as this is its first casualty.

Dorking and Leatherhead Advertiser 28 October 1916

Thomas Ernest Belton

Thomas is remembered at the Thiepval Memorial and on Fetcham War Memorial.

JAMES HENRY BROWNING – A Victorian Soldier

James first served his country in the late Nineteenth Century, swearing his allegiance to Queen Victoria and continued his service into World War One. He was baptised in St Mary's Church, Fetcham on 10 October 1876, the son of Charles and Sarah. The 1881 Census showed Charles as a fifty-five-year-old agricultural labourer born in Byfleet and Sarah, who was born in Fetcham was fifty, living with them in Cobham Road was their twenty-four-year-old son John a gardener, Daniel a twenty-two-year-old groom, thirteen-year-old agricultural labourer Charles, twelve-year-old Sarah, eight-year-old William and James himself, a four-year-old. Sarah, his mother, died in 1890 and the 1891 census recorded Charles as a widower working as a shepherd at Roaring House Farm on Fetcham Downs, near Bocketts Farm and fourteen-year-old James was a domestic gardener.

Postcard of Roaring House Farm 1934.

On 25 October 1893 James joined the 3rd Queen's Royal West Surrey Regiment, Service Number 8109 signing up for a period of six years. He was eighteen at the time and a gardener employed by Sir E G Moon at The Rectory, Fetcham. He was five feet five inches tall, with dark completion, brown hair and grey eyes with a thirty-five-inch chest. He was transferred to the Royal Artillery on the 6 December that year. On 1 July 1899, the Royal Artillery was divided into three groups: the Royal Horse Artillery of 21 batteries and the Royal Field Artillery of 95 batteries comprised one group, while the coastal defence, mountain, siege and heavy batteries were split off into another group named the Royal Garrison Artillery of 91 companies.

James was to marry in August 1903 at which time he was a twenty-eight-year-old soldier living at Okehampton Camp in Devon. His bride was Edith Gertrude Rigby of Fetcham and several members of the Gravett family were witnesses to the event. His father Charles died early in 1907. The 1911 Census recorded James as a thirty-five-year-old soldier based at Okehampton Camp in Devon, where he was described as a Battery Sergeant Major.

James served with the 14th Battery Royal Field Artillery and on 8 May 1915 the *Dorking and Leatherhead Advertiser* reported: *'Promotion: James Browning RFA has received a Lieutenant's Commission. He was born in the Parish (Fetcham) and educated at the school. He has served for 21 years. He went through the South African War, where he received the Distinguished Service Medal for Gallantry on the Battlefield and has attained the rank of Sergeant Major. We congratulate Lieut. Browning on this recognition of his services and his strict attention to duty.'*

A letter was also published entitled *'Fetcham Men and the War'* and read as follows: *'(To the Editor). Sir, - I should be glad if you will allow me to offer heartiest congratulations to Lieut. James Browning, who I see by the Parish Magazine has attained the above rank in strict devotion to duty. He was severely wounded in the South African War, where he served his gun until all the ammunition he could get was expended. I think every inhabitant should be, and is, proud of the men of Fetcham. Both rich and poor have responded to their country's call most nobly. – An old inhabitant.'*

The Distinguished Service Order is a high award for meritorious or distinguished service rather than an act of gallantry, although in many cases during 1914-1918 it is not easy to discriminate between these two reasons for granting an award; in some cases, it appears that a DSO was awarded when perhaps a full recommendation for a VC could not be justified or corroborated. All awards of the DSO were announced in the London Gazette, usually with a citation.

10896 SUPPLEMENT TO THE LONDON GAZETTE, 19 DECEMBER 1914

Battery Quartermaster-Serjeant S. B. Jenner.
Battery Serjeant-Major H. Birtles.
Battery Serjeant-Major Donald McCorquodale.
Battery Serjeant-Major James Browning.
Serjeant A. F. Jordan.

The Distinguished Service Medal. A silver medal, 36mm in diameter. The obverse bears the crowned effigy of the reigning monarch. The reverse has the inscription 'FOR DISTINGUISHED SERVICE'. The ribbon is dark blue and white.

Extract from The London Gazette 1914.

After the war the couple moved to South London and in 1930 were living in Scylla Road, Peckham.

FREDERICK CYRIL BUCKLAND

Frederick was born on 10 June 1890 in Burnham but by 1901 was living with his family in Leatherhead at Oak Lawn Lodge. His father George was a Gardener and Frederick was one of six children. The family continued to live at Oak Lawn Lodge and the 1911 Census showed Frederick was employed as a Carpenter. On 19 October 1912, he married Ethel Gertrude Gullick in Reigate Parish Church and their daughter Pamela was baptised on 2 May 1915 at St Mary's Church, Fetcham, at which time Frederick was described as a Woodsman.

Frederick enlisted on 10 December 1915 and served in both the 8th and 10th battalions The Queen's (Royal West Surrey) Regiment, Regimental Number G/13790. The 6th, 7th, 8th, 10th and 11th Service Battalions were made up of mainly Kitchener Volunteers. All of them served on the Western Front with distinction. The 8th lost heavily on the Western Front, particularly at the Somme and in the Third Battle of Ypres. The 10th and 11th were both with the 41st Division in 1916 and were decimated at Fleurs, but later contributed to the campaign in Italy. He was awarded the Silver War Badge, indicating that he had been wounded and was discharged on the 26 November 1918.

The 1919 Electoral Roll showed Frederick living at The Bungalow, Cobham Road, Fetcham. He died in August 1978 at which time his address was recorded as 296 Kingston Road, Leatherhead.

GAVIN RALSTON MURE CALDWELL

Gavin was born in 1897 and was the son of the Reverend William Henry McKennal Caldwell and Jessie Caldwell (nee Oxley). As with many familes of clergymen, they moved around the country and lived in Bagshott in 1901. By 1911 the family had taken up residence in St Augustine's Vicarage, Bristol and

Gavin Caldwell

Gavin attended Bristol Grammar School and later Clifton College.

In 1914, he joined the Officer Training Corps and was gazetted Second Lieutenant in the Argyll & Sutherland Highlanders on 21 October 1914. His family moved to Fetcham and his father became Rector at Fetcham and officiated at St Mary's Parish Church from November 1916 until April 1925. Gavin transferred to the Coldstream Guards in August 1916, and was sent to France in December of that year.

Gavin with his father Rev Caldwell

The Regiment's history goes back to 1650 when it was first formed at Berwick, Northumberland during the English Civil War, as part of the English Parliamentarian forces. Being the older Regiment it should have had seniority in the Household Troops but was placed as the second senior Regiment, after the 1st Regiment of Foot Guards. Subsequently it adopted the motto Nulli Secundus (Second to None), and always stands on the left of the line when on parade with rest of the Foot Guards. The regiment was involved in the Battle of Delville Wood and The Battle of the Ancre in 1916 and following the German retreat to the Hindenburg Line in 1917, took part in The First Battle of the Scarpe, the Battle of Arleux, The Second Battle of the Scarpe and The Battle of Cambrai.

Coldsream Guards Poster

Men of the Coldstream Guards with a captured German gun 1916

In 1918 the regiment was engaged in battles at St Quentin, Bapaume, Arras, Albert, Havrincourt,Canal du Nord and Cambrai. This battle took place in and around the French city of Cambrai between 8 and 10 October and incorporated many of the newer tactics of 1918, particularly tanks.

Gavin was wounded at the Battle of Cambrai, and died from his wounds on 9 October 1918 on reaching the dressing station. The War Diary for the '8th October reads ' *Trenches near RIBECOURT. The Battalion paraded at 10.00 a.m. and proceeded to trenches running North-West of MON PLAISIR FARM, near MASNIERES. 9th Trenches near MASBIERES. The Battalion paraded at 1.00 a.m. and marched to trenches West of SERANVILLIERS. The Battalion attacked at 4.30 a.m. and finally consolidated near CASTENIERES. Casualties:- Lieut G R M CALDWELL – KILLED 3 O.R's Killed, 4 O.R's Wounded and 2 O.R's Wounded (Remained at duty).'*

Gavin's grave is in the village cemetery at Wambaix a village some 10 kilometres south-south-east of Cambrai on the D142. He was twenty one years old and one of only five British soldiers buried there.

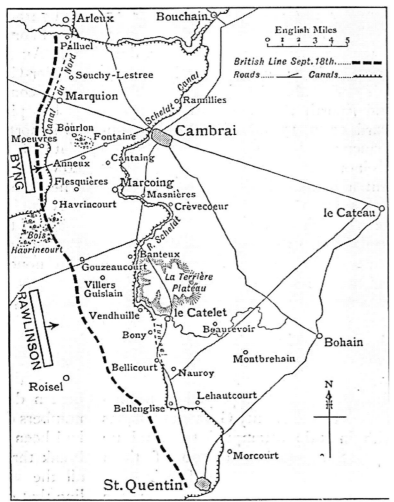

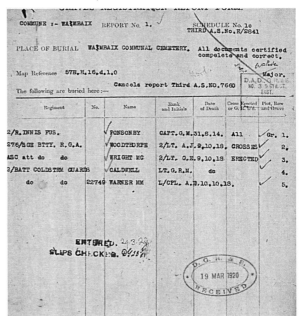

Gavin Caldwell burial record Wambaix Communal Cemetery, France

Map showing Masineres to the south of Cambrai.

Gavin Caldwell's headstone.

The 2 November 1918 edition of the *Surrey Advertiser* carried the following report of Gavin's Memorial Service held in Fetcham. It read - 'On Tuesday afternoon a special service was held at the Parish Church in memory of Lieut. Caldwell of the Coldstream Guards, only son of the Rector and Mrs Caldwell, whose death in France was recorded in our last issue. The service was conducted by the Reverend C M Jotcham, of Compton, and the clergy also present were Canon Hunter (Rural Dean), Reverend T F Hobson (Vicar of Leatherhead), and the Reverend C W Ingram. Among those present at the service were Mrs Caldwell, Mrs Hankey, Mr and Mrs C S Gordon Clark and others.'

Candlesticks and A Gold Watch

Mrs Jessie Caldwell was to leave three legacies in remembrance of her son Gavin. A pair of candlestick, a gift of a gold watch and a donation to Cuddesdon Theological College. The candlesticks were found in 2008 and given to Fetcham Church by Peter and Carmel Cauldfield-Key. When Carmel's brother died, they found the candlesticks amongst the military memorabilia which he had collected for many years. Carmel researched the history and found his name on the Fetcham War Memorial and decided to return them to Fetcham Church on Remembrance Day 2008.

Leonard Hammond was a stretcher bearer in the Coldstream guards and received the Military Medal for rescuing Gavin Caldwell from no man's land. Leonard and his fellow stretcher bearer were given watches by Gavin's mother, Jessie Caldwell, to thank them for their attempt to rescue her son.

Leonard was born in Norfolk in 1892 and enlisted in the Coldstream Guards in 1915.

When Mrs Jessie Caldwell died in 1936 'The Times' reported that she left £1,000 to the Cuddesdon Theological College, Wheatley, Oxford, in memory of her son.

Leonard Robert Hammond medals and photographs courtesy of Mark Hammond

FREDERIC J COOPER - The tale of Rubber Planting, Ostrich Farming and Elephant Shooting

Frederic was the son of Frances Cooper and was baptised in Great Bookham on 9 April 1882 but no father was shown in the Parish register. The 1891 Census showed nine-year-old Frederic living with his grandparents Henry and Annie Cooper (nee Cook) at Blacksmith's Cottage in Fetcham where Grandfather Henry, who was born in Dorking, was a forty-seven-year-old Blacksmith. Their son William was a Pupil Teacher and they had a twelve-year-old daughter Emma and nine-year-old son Robert.

Frederic travelled to East Africa in his early twenties, arriving in 1905 and was to describe himself as engaged in rubber planting, ostrich farming and elephant shooting. Towards the end of 1908 world rubber prices began to rise

and by October 1910 British companies had paid some £350,000 for 16,000 hectares of rubber plantations in German East Africa. The boom collapsed early in 1913. Ostrich farming was first set up in South Africa in 1863 and the fashion for ostrich plumes expanded rapidly until it peaked in about 1910, plumes, but then after faded.

Ostrich farm

The Surrey Advertiser dated 27 January 1917 carried an article entitled 'F J COOPER - 'FETCHAM MAN'S EXPERIENCES', it read –

'We have received a copy of the 'East African Standard', published in Nairobi, containing an account of the experiences of Mr F J Cooper, a native of Fetcham, while a prisoner in the hands of the Germans in East Africa. The account, written by Mr Cooper himself, occupies about 11 columns of the paper, and published in full, would fill six complete columns of the 'Surrey Advertiser'.

Mr Cooper's imprisonment dated from October 1st 1914 to September 20th 1916 on which latter date the Belgians marched into Tabora. During the long period of nearly two years the party of which Mr Cooper and his wife formed part were forced to march from place to place, were herded together in crowded, filthy and insanitary buildings, were subjected to almost every kind of insult, ill treatment and indignity, were denied proper food, medical attention and other necessities and were compelled to perform menial and disgusting tasks in the presence of the natives. It is a record which is an ineffaceable disgrace to the Germans, especially when it is known that ladies and clergymen were among those so treated.

There is one significant fact. When the Germans knew that the enemy were approaching, they were extremely anxious that British troops should arrive before the Belgians, evidently fearing the vengeance of the latter, but trusting to the known humanity and generosity of the former.

Mr Cooper had been in East Africa since 1905, engaged in rubber planting, ostrich farming and elephant shooting, and at the time of his internment was general manager of the Lewa Rubber Estates near Tanga, in which was then German East, but is now British.'

The 1918 Government Committee on the treatment by the enemy of British Prisoners of War in German East Africa stated -

'Very serious reports having reached His Majesty's Government with regard to the treatment by the Authorities in German East Africa of the British Civilian Prisoners of War there, the Committee were directed to collect all available

information upon the subject and report upon it for the information of the Secretary of State. This Report is the outcome of that direction. In one respect the task of preparing it has presented little difficulty. The information before the Committee is clear, precise, and, as they believe, quite reliable. The witnesses include planters and other British subjects who chanced to find themselves in the Colony at the outbreak of war, and the Committee have been specially assisted by the information supplied by the Clerical Missionaries.

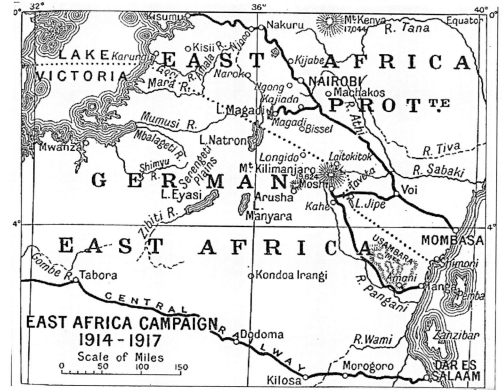

Map of the East African Campaign 1914-1917

On September 29th, 1914, orders were received from the German General Command that all English people in the Tanga District, Missionaries included, were to proceed forthwith on an eleven days' march to Morogoro, a hill town on the Central Railway, which, in December, 1914, became the seat of Government of the Colony. The principal places in which at one time or another the civilian prisoners were interned were Kilimatinde, Kiboriani, Buigiri and Tabora. These camps, as has been said, were located on or near the Central Railway.

KILIMATINDE, actually on the Central Railway, was, before the war, an old military post. The prisoners interned there were confined in a stone fort. They were permitted two hours' daily exercise in a space about 100 yards square, set out on the top of the hill on which the fort was built. Except for that indulgence they were not allowed to pass the gates, notwithstanding constant protest against the restriction. The camp was dirty and the sanitary arrangements quite inadequate. The Commandant was warned, but without avail, that an outbreak of typhoid must result from the insanitary conditions under which the prisoners were compelled to exist. Such an outbreak did supervene in December, 1915. It was only after it had passed that a slight improvement was even attempted. As to the food, this at first was good, but it gradually deteriorated. By November, 1914, it consisted of meat and bones, bread made from millet and very weak coffee without milk or sugar. In the early days, the prisoners were allowed to purchase small luxuries like fruit, etc., and they were permitted to order from Dar-es-Salaam or Tabora any clothes or other things of which they stood in need.

After the Battle of Tanga, however, in November 1914, says Reverend E F Spanton, whose mission station was at Msalabani, in the Tanga District of the Colony 'the attitude of the Germans towards us changed in a marked degree. Feeling secure of their future in the Colony, they began to bully the prisoners, withdrawing one by one the privileges we had been allowed, and subjecting us to a continually increasing number of regulations.'

'Punishments were of a particularly arbitrary kind. Prisoners, often without knowing, and constantly without any opportunity of meeting, the charge against them, were put in cells, most frequently in one designed for natives, and infested by vermin, with a low roof of corrugated iron, and with such an absence of ventilation that the heat in the middle of the day was overpowering. The Committee take as an example of this treatment the case of Mr Cooper, a British planter. He was confined in his cell for several days without any kind of trial. The only charge against him was that he had complained about the food, with what reason is not open to doubt. Representations addressed to the Commandant against the treatment of this man only evoked the reply that prisoners were not entitled to make complaints. As prisoners they had no rights, so it was said, and the Commandant added that in future any complaint *lodged by any number or body of them would be treated as a revolt and dealt with as such.'* (British civilian prisoners in German East Africa – a report. Great Britain. Government Committee on Treatment by the Enemy of British Prisoners of War Printed by Alabaster, Passmore & Sons Date Issued: 1918)

Whilst it cannot be confirmed that this is our Frederick Cooper, it is a likely supposition.

HENRY REGINALD COOPER

Henry was born on 5 August and baptised on 2 September 1900 at St Mary's Church, Fetcham. He was the son of Fetcham born Charles Cooper, a Gardener and Georgina (nee Simmonds) who was born in Great Bookham. In 1911 Henry lived in Stoke Road with his parents and elder brother William Charles who was born in 1898.

The School Log Book indicated that Henry left school aged fourteen on the 7 August 1914. On 20 August 1918, as an eighteen-year-old gardener standing five feet four inches tall, he enlisted in the Middlesex Regiment 53rd Young Soldier Battalion. Up to 27 October 1917, this was known as 102nd Young Soldier Battalion and had no regimental affiliation. Before that it had been 28th (Reserve) Battalion of the Middlesex Regiment - a basic recruit training unit based at Aldershot and part of the 23rd Reserve Brigade. In 1925, Henry married Mary Ann Watchorn. He passed away in 1956.

THE DIMENTS

The First World War had a huge impact on many local families such as the Diments. Families who had already known sadness and loss were torn apart as their young men went off to fight.

William Diment was born in Dorset in 1842 and was an agricultural labourer married to Eliza Strudwick, born in Fetcham in 1855. The couple married on 4 August 1878 at St Mary's Church, Fetcham.

St Mary's Church, Fetcham

Barrack's Farm shown in the background

Eliza gave birth to ten children; her first child Emily was registered under her mother's maiden name before William and Eliza were married. The 1881 census located the family in Woodland Cottages, Stoke D'Abernon, the 1891 census showed them living at Barracks Farm, Fetcham.

Eliza died around the time of the birth of her son Albert in early 1897. Albert had four older brothers and five older sisters and yet he found himself in the workhouse with his widowed father in 1904 for fifty days. The Epsom Union Workhouse register stated that William died on the fifty first day of his admission, he was listed as a shepherd aged sixty-four. On the day, his father died Albert was discharged into the care of Mrs Longhurst, his sister.

The Epsom Union Workhouse

Fetcham School pupils were photographed separately in the 1890's. It is likely the boys pictured include John Henry Diment and William James Diment. Rose Diment is the firth girl from the left in the middle row.

All five Diment boys served during the conflict. John with the Royal Fusiliers, William as a Corporal with the Royal Engineers, Maurice, with the Queen's Royal West Surrey's and Royal Engineers, David with the Army Service Corps and Albert with the Queen's Royal West Surreys.

Girls at Fetcham School 1890's. Rose Diment fifth girl from the left in middle row

Grace Diment was born in 1882 and married George Stovell of Leatherhead on 25 November 1899, two years after the death of her mother. The 1911 census shows Grace and George had two children, Rose and George. George Senior was a stockman living and working at Fetcham Common. Their daughter Rose Stovell was to serve with the Women's Royal Army Auxiliary Corps during World War One.

John Henry Diment was born in 1884 and was only thirteen when his mother died. The 1911 census showed him working as a Groom at the Kennels Stables in Great Bookham. John was attested for service with the Royal Fusiliers in December 1915 and mobilised on 24 May 1915 and served in France, later transferring to the 101st Labour Corp as Private 60117. His service records survived the Nazi bombings during World War Two. The Labour Corp was formed in January 1917 and grew to some 389,900 men (more than 10% of the total size of the Army) by the Armistice. Of this total, around 175,000 were working in the United Kingdom and the rest in the theatres of war. The Corps was manned by officers and other ranks who had been medically rated below the 'A' condition needed for front line service. Many were returned wounded. Labour Corps units were often deployed for work within the range of enemy guns, sometimes for lengthy periods.

As a Royal Fusilier, it is likely John took part in the Battles of the Somme. John suffered from gas poisoning whilst on active service and returned to England in May 1918 where he died as a result of gas poisoning and pneumonia at St Luke's War Hospital, in Halifax. His sister Grace was listed as John's next of Kin and his body was brought back to Fetcham and buried at St Mary's on 28 May 1918. John was thirty-eight years old.

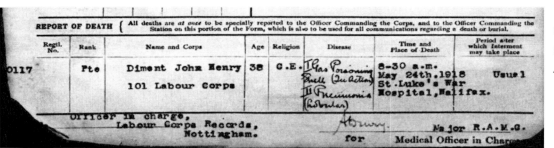

Labour Corps Records, Nottingham — death of John Diment.

St Luke's War Hospital, Halifax

William James Diment was born in April 1885 and baptised in Fetcham on 30th May at St Mary's Parish Church. The 1891 and 1901 census showed him living at Barracks Farm with his family. Upon leaving school he worked as a 'cow boy on farm'. In 1910, he married Julia Perry from Dorking. The 1911 census showed the couple living in Eastwick Street in Great Bookham with their five-month-old son William George. The couple went on to have a daughter Ellen Margaret born in March 1913.

William's medal index card showed he served as Corporal 160730 with the Royal Engineers and then as Corporal WR/255263 (the WR representing waterways and railways).

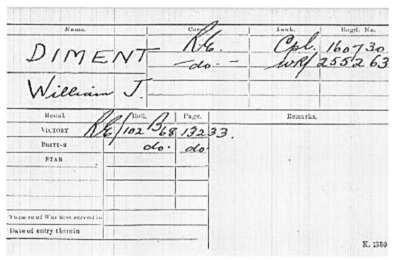

William was awarded the British and Victory Medals which indicates he served overseas during the conflict but not until at least 1915. The first of the railway operating companies were raised in April of 1915 and deployed to France in June of that year. They performed three basic functions including the management of traffic, provision of crews for locomotives and the repair of rolling stock and other items needed to keep a railway in operation.

William and Fanny moved to East Flexford, near Guildford and had two further daughters, Julia born in June 1919 and Elsie May in 1927. William died in 1974 and is buried at St Mary the Virgin Church, Worplesdon.

Maurice Diment was baptised at St Mary's in May 1888, he was nine years old when his mother died and only sixteen when his father passed away. The 1911 census located Maurice with the Queen's Royal West Surrey Regiment as a 'servant to officers' at the Stoughton Barracks just outside Guildford.

The Queen's Royal West Surrey Regiment 1st Battalion musters 1,000 soldiers in August 1914, just before it is deployed to France

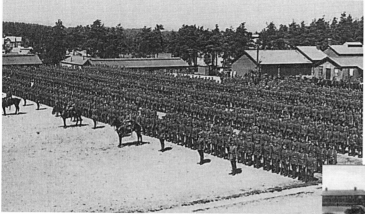

Maurice was not awarded the 1914-15 Star Medal which suggests that he did not go to France with the regiment at the beginning of the war. He did however serve overseas with the Queen's Regiment and later with the Royal Engineers. In 1922, he married Florence Miles and two years later their daughter Eva was born in Farnham. At this time, Maurice was still a serving soldier.

In early September 1926 Maurice, Florence and Eva boarded the P & O steamship *Borde* to Freemantle in Australia. Alongside them on their journey to a new life were Maurice's fellow soldiers, all of whom had been in vocational training at the Catterick Army Camp in Richmond, North Yorkshire. Maurice died in Perth in 1955 aged 77.

Postcard of Catterick Camp

Eleanor Diment was born in 1890 and around the age of fourteen she became an orphan. The 1911 census showed Eleanor as a twenty-one-year-old servant to the family of John Johnson, a wine and spirit merchant, living at Station Road, Redhill. On 19 June 1915, she married Henry Jones from Croydon who was fourteen years her senior. Eleanor died in 1970.

David Cornelius Diment (christened Cornelius) was born in Fetcham in July 1891 and baptised on 30 August. He grew up with his siblings at Barracks Farm. On 1 August 1909 David fell from a stable loft and damaged his leg. Once his parents had died David boarded with his sister Rose and worked as a farm labourer. On 12 December 1915, two days after his brother John, David enlisted to join the army and was posted with the Army Service Corp's Motor Transport,

his service number 169048. In 1915 David saw active service with the Army Service Corp in France, although he was home on 2 September 1915, shortly after the death of his younger brother Albert. David's leg had never truly healed from his fall in 1910, so much so he found himself in front of an army medical board on 7 April 1917. David was medically discharged from the army, suffering from an ulcerated left leg, on 28 April 1917. Although only twenty-four years he was considered 25% unfit for employment and was issued with a Silver War Badge.

Army Service Corps

In November 1917 David married Lucy Payne, his brother Maurice was a witness at his wedding. Lucy was a domestic servant who lived in Leatherhead. The 1939 Register showed David and Lucy lived at 32 Church Walk, Leatherhead with David working as a gardener. He died in September 1963.

May Beatrice Diment was born in 1894, three years before her mother died. In 1901 six-year-old May went to live with her uncle and aunt, George and Annie Friday at their home at Redland Cottages, Holmwood. George Friday was a woodman. By the time May was sixteen she had gone into service for the Hylton-Foster family of Old Dene, Bookham. Their son Sir Harry Braustbyn Hylton-Foster then aged six years, was to become the British Conservative Party Politian who served as a Member of Parliament and The Speaker of the House of Commons until his death in 1950. There is a marriage record of a May B Diment marrying Henry Butler in Horsham in 1941.

Albert Diment was the youngest of the Diment children, born in 1897. His mother died at the time of his birth. In 1904 Albert joined his father in the Epsom Union Workhouse for 51 days before leaving as an orphan. Upon their father's death, Albert's sister Rose Longhurst took Albert from the workhouse and provided him with a home.

Discharge Book Epsom Union Workhouse November 1904 Albert Diment

Albert enlisted in Guildford as Private G/2317 with the 7th Battalion of the Queen's Royal West Surrey Regiment. He first went to France with the Regiment on 26 July 1915, which entitled him to the 1915 Star, British and Victory medals. Albert died on the 13 July 1916 during the Battles of the Somme although the Surrey Advertiser 14 October 1916 reported him "wounded and missing" The newspaper reports that before enlisting Albert lived with his sister in Fetcham and was employed as a cowman by Mrs Hansard of Millfield, Cobham.

Surrey Advertiser 14 October 1916.

A further newspaper article dated 13 January 1917 referred to a letter received by Miss Diment of Bookham, from Captain J S Walter concerning her brother, who had been missing since 13 July. He said he was afraid that her brother 'died with so many others on that terrible day'. He was reported wounded, but there were some who believed he had been killed. He added that Private Diment was a brave lad, who always did his duty, and was always among the first to volunteer for anything dangerous.

Surrey Advertiser 13 January 1917

The war diary for the Royal West Surreys showed that Albert was caught up in the attack on Trones Wood on 13 July 1916. Trones Wood lay on the northern slopes of Montauban ridge, between Bernafay Wood and Guillemont. The wood dominated the southern approach to Longueval and Trones Alley, a German communication trench between Bernafay Wood and the northern tip of Trones Wood to Guillemont. The wood was pear-shaped, with a base about 400 yards (366m) wide on Montauban ridge, the rest of the wood running north for about 1,400 yards (1,280m), coming to a point on a rise towards Longueval village. The wood had dense undergrowth which retarded movement, made it difficult to keep direction and during the battle the trees were brought down by shell-fire, becoming entangled with barbed-wire and strewn with German and British dead. The British attacks were part of preliminary operations, to reach ground from which to begin the second British general attack of the Battle of the Somme, against the German second position from Longueval to Bazantin la Petit on 14 July.

1916.

July.

13th
(Contd)

where he met Officers Commanding Companies – Orders for attack of Northern Portion of TRONES WOOD at 7 p.m. were then issued – See Appendix III Brigade operation orders were received at 4 p.m. Company Commanders returned to their commands and issued instructions. Leading Coy moved forward from DUBLIN TRENCH at 5.30 p.m. Battn was greatly impeded by a relief moving up into LONGUEVAL ALLEY at the same time – At 7 p.m. Battn assaulted TRONES WOOD from Northern extremity over a front of 750 yards – One Company of 7th Buffs detailed to assist Battn in the assault, became much disorganised owing to casualties caused by Shell fire when moving up to the attack and only about one and a half platoons arrived in time to partake in the assault. Battn H.Q. arrived in LONGUEVAL ALLEY at 7 p.m. (ZERO hour). Battn, on assaulting was met by very heavy rifle, machine gun & Shell fire and the advance was definitely checked owing to no supporting troops being to hand – The enemy would appear to have suffered very little damage from our bombardment as he developed very heavy rifle fire – The enemy also barraged on LONGUEVAL ALLEY – At 8.50 p.m. a message was received that Northern Portion of TRONES WOOD would be rebombarded & that attack was not to be pressed if success seemed unlikely – At 9 p.m. remainder of battn & 7th Buffs reorganised for defence of LONGUEVAL ALLEY in conjunction with present garrison – At 12.30 a.m. 14th July instructions were received that Battn might withdraw to German old front line system if LONGUEVAL ALLEY was sufficiently held – At 2.30 a.m. Battn withdrew to BEDFORD TRENCH – Casualties, officers 13, O.R. 216. xxxx (For details see Appen: IV

Z 2 SUB-SECTION & BILLON VALLEY BROWTOWN CAMP.

Appen: III
Report on
action –

Appendix
IV
Casualties
of Battn
July 13
1916.

War Diary Queen's Royal West Surrey July 1916

Graves in Trones Wood just after the War.

The site of Guillemont village during the War

Nineteen-year-old Albert Diment is listed on the Thiepval Memorial to the Missing of the Somme battlefields. The memorial bears the names of 72,194 officers and men of the United Kingdom and South African forces.

Albert and John were not alive to witness the Armistice of 11 November 1918 between the Allies and Germany to end the fighting on the Western Front. It was a victory for the Allies but for the remaining members of the Diment family must have been a bitter sweet moment. The two Diment brothers are remembered alongside each other on Fetcham War Memorial.

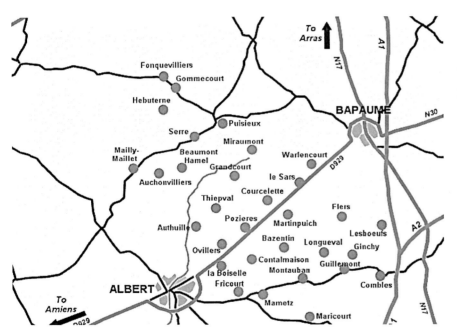

The Somme, France – Front Line 1 July – 19 November 1916.

First Phase	Second Phase	Third Phase
1st- 13th July: Battle of Albert	14th - 17th July: Bazentin Ridge	15th - 22nd Sept: Flers - Courcelette
1st July: Gommecourt	19th July: Fromelles	25th- 28th Sept: Morval
	15th July - 9th Sept: Deville Wood	26th- 28th Sept: Thiepval
	20th - 25th July High Wood	1st- 18th Oct: Le Transloy
	23rd July - 3rd Sept : Pozieres	1st Oct - 11th Nov: Ancre Heights
	3rd - 6th Sept: Guillemont	13th - 18th Nov: Ancre
	9th Sept: Ginchy	

GEORGE WILLIAM EASDOWN

George was baptised on the 31 March 1889 in Fetcham and was the son of Walter, a gardener and Mary. The couple lived in Cobham Road and had an elder son Charles Walter who was two years George's senior. In 1901, the family are found living in a row of cottages in Stoke Road, but by 1911 they had moved to 3 Pretoria Cottages, Kingston Road, Leatherhead, where the occupations of Walter and his two unmarried sons was given as Gardeners.

George went on to serve as a Private T/4675 and 202244 in the 1/4th The Queen's (Royal West Surrey) Regiment which served in India from 29 October 1914, remaining there throughout the war. At the end of the war George was awarded the British and Victory Medals. He married Alice Sharp in May 1928. His death was recorded in February 1960.

Queen's (Royal West Surrey) Regiment in India 1915

ARTHUR FREEMAN – A PRISONER OF WAR Arthur was born in Steyning, Sussex in 1891 but by 1901 at the age of ten he was living with his parents Peter and Emily (nee Chatfield Herbert) in Moors Cottage, Fetcham. His father Peter was a Miller and Arthur's fifteen-year-old brother Ernest was a butcher, who unfortunately died seven years later at the age of twenty-three. His fourteen-year-old brother Charles was a Telegraph Messenger and Arthur was to later work as a builder's labourer and baker.

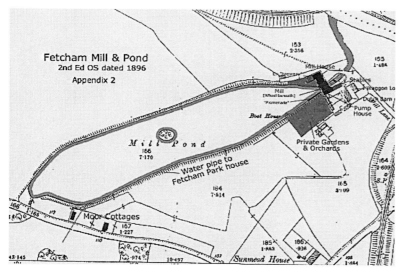

Moor Cottages, Cobham Road - demolished circa 1930 (Leatherhead & District History Society)

'The Moor or Moore Cottages were alongside Cobham Road and took their name from their location, being once known as 'the Moor' (here meaning marshy ground). They were in separate small enclosures, and by 1851 had grown to being three in number. But only two survived into the 20th century to be replaced by semi-detached houses built around 1930. (Alan Pooley, LDLHS)'

Arthur's military service record showed he served with the 3rd battalion, Machine Gun Corp and that he passed a medical examination in Leatherhead on the 27 May 1915. His occupation was given as a Baker and he was five foot five inches tall and had a chest measurement of thirty-nine inches with four childhood vaccination marks on his arm. He was twenty-four years old at the time. Mr A W Wild a Baker and Confectioner of Bridge Street, Leatherhead was to provide a character reference, describing him as 'steady, honest and industrious, clean in his person and work.'

He embarked at Folkestone on 21 July 1917 and arrived in Boulogne where he joined the MGC (Machine Gun Corps) base at Camiers. During the First World War the flat lands around Etaples were the site of the huge base depot of the British army in France. It is usually known nowadays as Étaples camp. Through most of the war, close to it and part of the same complex, Camiers camp was base depot in France of the Machine Gun Corps. Its home depot was at Belton Park, near Grantham.

A machine gun post

The British Army adopted the Vickers gun as its standard machine gun on 26 November 1912, using it alongside their Maxims. However, there were still shortages when the First World War began, and the British Expeditionary Force was still equipped with Maxims when sent to France in 1914. Vickers was threatened with prosecution for war profiteering, due to the high price it was demanding for each gun. As a result, the price was slashed. As the war progressed, and numbers increased, it became the British Army's primary machine gun, and served on all fronts during the war. When the Lewis Gun was adopted as a light machine gun and issued to infantry units, the Vickers guns were redefined as heavy machine guns, and withdrawn from infantry units, and passed to the new Machine Gun Corps. After the First World War, the Machine Gun Corps (MGC) was disbanded.

Arthur was posted missing on the 5 April 1918 and taken prisoner.

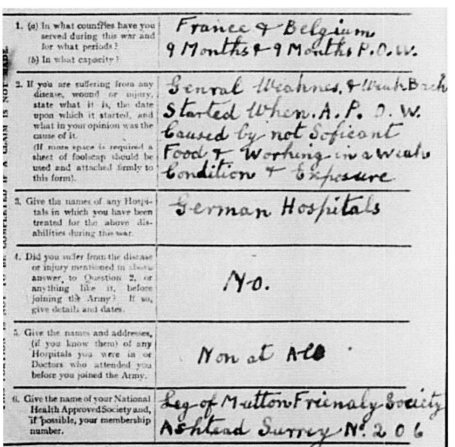

Prisoner of First World War Records International Committee of the Red Cross

He returned to England on 1 January 1919 and was subsequently discharged on 1 April 1919 and transferred to the Reserves. He stated he had in served in France and Belgium and had been a Prisoner of War for nine months and suffered a general weakness and weak back which had started when he was an Allied Prisoner of War (APOW) because of insufficient food, exposure and working in a weak condition. He also stated he had been treated in German hospitals.

Arthur Freeman's Service Record

Further records revealed he was examined at Horton (County of London) War Hospital in Epsom but no disability found. He complained of pains in his back and that he perspired and became short of breath on exertion. The medical examiners recorded 'Present condition: An exceptionally strong and well-nourished man who looks the picture of health. Heart appeared normal. There is nothing abnormal to be found on examination of lungs and abdominal organs. Pathologists report on urine attached shows no abnormality. His exercise tolerance was found to be very good. Weight 12st. 10lbs'. The report was dated 24 July 1919.

The records also refer to the fact he had taken out insurance with a National Health Approved Society called the Leg of Mutton Friendly Society after the Leg of Mutton Inn in Ashtead, where its members met. It operated a clothing club, coal club, penny bank and burial club. The printed rules of the club, which survive from 1895, state that the society's object was 'to provide by voluntary subscriptions of the members for the relief or maintenance of the members during sickness or other infirmity, whether bodily or mental; for insuring money to be paid on the death of a member, or for the funeral expenses of a wife of a member. Membership was open to any man aged between 16 and 40 and each prospective member was required to produce a medical certificate certifying that he was 'of sound constitution' at the time of joining. It cost 2s. 6d. to join the society and then 2s. per month.   In the event of sickness or injury (other than brought on himself by 'debauched or irregular practices') a member would receive 12s. a week for up to six months and then 6s. a week for the next six months. Those claiming sickness benefit might be subjected to a medical examination. At the end of each year any profits remaining to the club were divided between the members. On the death of a member each member paid 1s. towards the cost of his funeral or 6d on the death of a member's wife. Members were excluded if convicted of any crime or if found to be 'of a drunken, quarrelsome disposition, or much given to fighting'.   A 3d. fine was payable for swearing, gambling or carrying 'any liquor out of the room to drink'; a 1s. fine was payable for talking about the society's affairs to non-members or for provoking discord.'

Some five years later in April 1924 Arthur married Dora May Sopp at St Peter's Church in Woking.   They were to have three children. He died in 1980.

ALBERT ERNEST GRAVETT and Family

Albert was baptised on 27 December 1896 in St Mary's Church, Fetcham. He had two elder sisters, nine-year-old Sarah and eight-year-old Ella, and an older brother William who was five at the time of his birth. His parents John and Emily Elizabeth (nee Browning) Gravett had lived in the grounds of Fetcham Lodge, where John was employed as a Gardener, since their marriage in 1891. The 1911 Census referred to John as the Head Gardener and the couple had

Gravett family 1911 Census

had thirteen children by this time, although only eleven had survived. The June 1930 Auction Sale Documents for Fetcham Lodge estate, described the Head Gardener's Cottage as brick built and slated and part tiled and containing a Sitting Room, Kitchen, Scullery, Two Bedrooms, Two Attics and a Bath room with WC.   The census described Albert's mother Emily's occupation as 'Home Duties' and their eldest daughter nineteen-year-old Sarah was employed as a kitchen maid, whilst sixteen-year-old son William had followed his father's profession and was a gardener. Albert himself was described as a carpenter's assistant. Mildred, Hilda, Henry, Lawrence, Arthur, Frederick and two-year-old Rose, made up the younger members of family.

Albert Gravett VAD Record Card

Three years after the census Albert's eldest brother William emigrated to Canada, arriving in Quebec in May 1914. By October 1914, with the first casualties returning from the Front, Albert was working part time at the Red House Auxiliary Hospital as a Private in the 17 VAD Surrey where he completed 151 hours of duty before leaving in March 1915. His duties as an Orderly included detraining wounded at Clandon Park Hospital. The Red House Hospital tended to offer medical assistance to Belgium soldiers and Albert would also have been aware of the Belgian refugees staying in Leatherhead. These experiences may have inspired him to sign up before conscription to help out the abused Belgians and as a result of the sights of wounded soldiers he had helped carry into the hospital at Clandon. His address on the record was shown The Bungalow, Surrey Gardens, Cobham, previously Fetcham Lodge.

He enlisted on 20 April 1915 when his occupation was described as Blacksmith and was discharged on completion of twelve years' service on 19 April 1927. His military medal card showed that he served in the Royal Field Artillery Regimental number 95766, Highland Light Infantry Regimental Number 21006, and the Machine Gun Corps, Regimental Number 7732. During the conflict a man wishing to join the regular army could do so providing he passed certain physical tests and was willing to enlist for a number of years. The recruit had to be taller than 5 feet 3 inches and aged between 18 and 38 (although he could not be sent overseas until he was aged 19). He would join at the Regimental Depot or at one of its normal recruiting offices. Albert would have had a choice over the regiment he was assigned to. He would typically join the army for a period of seven years' full time service with the colours, to be followed by another five in the Army Reserve. (These terms were for infantry: the other arms had slightly different ones. For example, in the artillery it was for 6 years plus 6).

He initially joined the Royal Field Artillery before moving onto the Highland Light Infantry where he proved himself a very good shot. Only soldiers showing a talent for use of a rifle were chosen to go into the Machine Gun Corps. The records suggest he was promoted to Corporal when he was with the Machine Gun Corp - once again showing he was a sound soldier who could take on responsibility at a young age.

Royal Field Artillery

The creation of the MGC in October 1915 incorporated the Motor Machine Gun Service, which became known as the Machine Gun Corps (Motors). At this time, the MGC(M) had around 3000 men. From late 1916, many men of the MGC(M) transferred to the Heavy Section, MGC (later to be known as the Tank Corps). In 1922, the Tank Corps absorbed the MGC(M) completely and the Motor Machine guns' units disappeared from the British army's order of battle.

Machine Gun Corps Recruitment Poster

The MGC saw action in all the main theatres of war, including France, Belgium, Palestine, Mesopotamia, Egypt, Salonika, East Africa and Italy. In its short history, the MGC gained an enviable record for heroism as a front-line fighting force. Indeed, in the latter part of the war, as tactics changed to defence in depth, it commonly served well in advance of the front line. It had a less enviable record for its casualty rate. Some 170,500 officers and men served in the MGC with 62,049 becoming casualties, including 12,498 killed, earning it the nickname 'the Suicide Club'. When the first tanks were produced in 1916, they were manned by members of the Machine Gun Corps, formed into six companies which were collectively known as the Heavy Branch. The very first battle involving tanks took place on the Somme.

Machine Gun Crew wearing anti-gas helmets

Original British WWI Fluted Vickers Machine Gun

A Mark 1 tank on the Somme in 1916. The trailing wheels, meant to assist steering, were soon found to be more of a hindrance than a help and were eliminated from subsequent models.

This cartoon is typical of the late 1917-1918 period.

Albert was finally discharged from the army on completion of twelve years' service on 19 April 1927.

| 7807253 | R Gravett | Albert Ernest | 20.4.15 | 18¾ | Guildford | from M.G.C 7.6.21 | Blacksmith | 9.4.21 | 6 6.21 | Feltham Leatherhead Surrey | James Robertson W Adam B) |

Place of Marriage, and of Birth of each Child	Date of Marriage, and of Birth of each Child	Campaigns, Wounds, Medals or Rewards of any kind	Discharge or becoming Non Effective			Rank and Character on Discharge	Rate of pension awarded (if any)	Address on Discharge	Particulars of Former Service giving Corps and Number	Remarks
			Date	Place	Cause					
	26.12.20	The St War France 1916-19 British War Medal. Victory Medal.	18.7.19	Yorks S.W.	To Sect. B.	Sgt V. Good		8 Paradise Row Whitehall Taunton.	M.G.C. No 7808705.	DOB 70 EXETER 12/7/35
	1.4.23 14.11.25		29.1.24	Hampton Court	Section D. A. Res	Sgt.				
			23.1.28	Barnet	Discharged	V. Good				
Eltham Kent	27.12.21	The St Wes France 5.12.14 to 1919 1914-1915 STAR. British War Medal. Victory Medal.	18.8.20	Yorks S.W.	To Sect. B	Corporal Exemplary			M.G.C No 7807831	
			30.8.24	Hampton Court.		Cpl Exemplary		Royal Enclosure Ascot. Berks.		
Fetcham	9.7.31	The St Wes France 1916-19 British War Medal. Victory Medal.	30.5.19	York St S.W.	To Sect B	Corporal Very Good		The Bungalow Surry Gardens Cobham Surrey.	M.G.C No 7807253	
			19.4.27	Barnett.	Discharged	Sgt. V. Good				
		The St War France 1914-17 1914 STAR	5.7.19	York St S.W.	To Section B.			2 Chromston Road	M.G.C	

Albert Gravett Discharge Papers

Albert's brother Henry, who was four years younger, served with the Queen's Royal West Surrey and also the Labour Corps, whilst his older brother William now living in Canada was to serve with the Canadian Overseas Expeditionary Force during the conflict.

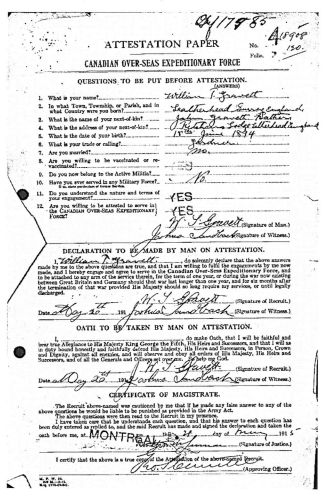

William Gravett's Attestation Paper Canadian Overseas Expeditionary Force

In 1921 Albert married Janet Robinson McAdam in St Mary's Church, Fetcham at which time he was employed as a Chauffeur and lived at Fetcham Lodge. Albert's father John died on 1 February 1922 aged fifty six, he had worked for forty one years as Gardener at Fetcham Lodge. Albert and Janet had one child, a son John was born the following year on 23 August 1923.

Albert Gravett's son John

Another of Albert's brothers, Arthur Richard although too young to serve in World War One enlisted in the East Surrey Regiment on 28 August 1922 when he was eighteen. He is shown in the Fetcham School Log book leaving school in November 1917 for farm work.

44

9 Nov. Weekly Average 663 = 92%. 72 on books Thomas Oliver has left.

16. Mr Budd transplanted three apple trees, which have been budded and grafted as lessons by the horticultural class, from the seed bed in the gardens to a site near the tool shed.

The Rector is absent on chaplain duty. Weekly Average 67.8 = 94.1%. 72 on books Arthur Gravett aged 14. left for farm work. Nurse Dominy visited yesterday and reported all clean.

Arthur Gravett School Log Book 1917

He served his country in World War Two when he became a Warrant Officer class II CSM in the 1st battalion the East Surrey Regiment. He was mentioned in despatches and sadly lost his life on the 16 November 1940 aged thirty six. He is remembered at the Lockerbie (Drufesdale) Cemetery.

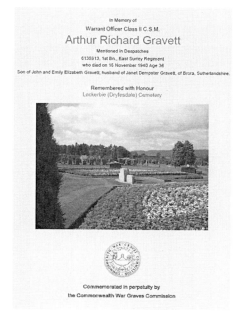

Arthur Richard Gravett Commonweath War Graves Commission Lockerbie

Albert's mother Emily Elizabeth died in 1937 when she was seventy two and was buried with her husband in St Mary's Churchyard.

L to R Jestina Florence Killick, Jestina Gravett (nee) McAdam, Robert Sydney Killick, Albert Ernest Gravett

Albert passed away in Buckinghamshire in 1968, his wife Janet's death was recorded in 1985.

BERTIE HAMES

Bertie Hames was baptised at Holy Trinity, Hampstead on the 30 September 1877. His father Mortimer was a coachman and his mother was Elizabeth Ann (nee Chadwell). As a two year, old he lived at 2 William Mews, Belsize Lane, St John, Hampstead but by the time he was twelve the family were living at Ealing. In 1901 Bertie, now twenty-two, was boarding in Twickenham and employed as a Grocer's Assistant. He married Helena Mary Ridgers from Windlesham, in 1907 in Chertsey.

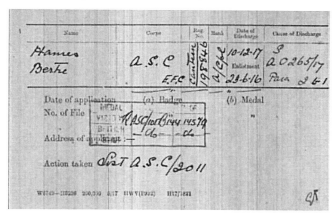

The couple lived in Stoke Road, Fetcham in 1911 where their two sons, Wilfred aged two and one year old Albert, were born. On 23 June 1916 at the age of thirty-six, Bertie enlisted in the Army Service Corps, Regimental number Canteen 198846. He was discharged on 10 December 1917. Bertie died on 11 June 1941 at the age of sixty-three in Chichester, Sussex.

Medal Card for Bertie Hames

JOHN BARNARD HANKEY and Family – The Lord of the Manor

The Hankey family became owners of Fetcham Park House in 1788 greatly benefiting the social needs of the village and the welfare of the inhabitants, both financially and by employing many as household servants, gardeners and agricultural labourers working on the adjoining farms and land.

John Barnard Hankey was born on 21 April 1845 at Fetcham Park and educated at Eton and Oxford. He married Fanny Helen Pratt Barlow in April 1872 and inherited Fetcham Park some three years later at the age of thirty.

Fetcham Park

He commissioned a leading architect to undertake a complete facelift of the house and the family moved to Eaton House, London where they are shown with their four children George, Dorothea, Edward, Mary, and thirteen servants in the 1881 census, whilst the work was undertaken. Cicely was born later that year and a sixth child Francis was born in 1886 but Fanny died on the 19 December of that year a fortnight after her confinement and was buried at Fetcham on 23 December. The couple had been married for thirteen years.

In April 1888, John married his second wife, twenty eight year old Ellen Gertrude Moon, the daughter of Reverend Sir Edward Graham Moon, Rector of Fetcham for fifty years.   The couple had three children, Thomas born in 1889, Arthur in 1890 and a daughter Miriam in 1892. All five of John's sons went on to be educated at Eton, and the four eldest were to serve with distinction in the forthcomlng war.   The 1910 Finance Act illustrated the extent of the Hankey's interests in the village with John listed as landlord of many properties, including land and cottages at Cannon Court Farm, Chain Cottage, numerous cottages in Cobham Road, including New Cottages, Pound Cottage, Well Meadow, Dower Cottage in The Street, cottages in Bell Lane, Fetcham Lodge, Forge Cottage, Home Farm in The Street, Mill House and Mill Meadow, Moor Cottages, cottages in River Lane, Roaring House Farm, Sunnyside in Cobham Road, The Bell PH, The Post Office cottage, The Saltbox, The Well House. He was master of the Surrey Union Foxhounds from 1876 to 1882, and became High Sheriff of Surrey in 1879 and also acted as a Justice of the Peace. He enjoyed the races at Epsom and Sandown and would hold house parties during the shooting season with pheasants, partridges and hares in abundance.

John also had interests in Canada and in the early 1900's, bought the Fairmont Hot Springs Ranch from its original owner, Sam Brewer. He offered accommodation for $2 per day, which included use of the hot springs. With the construction of the bathhouse (or "palatial sanitarium" as it was described), the resort staked its claim as a hub of health, wellness and hospitality. He sold the ranch and roadhouse in 1912.

Early photo of Fairmount Hot Spring Ranch

John passed away on 24 May 1914 in Fetcham at the age of sixty nine , after being married for the second time for a further twenty six years. (Extracts from fieldtrial.in/family tree).

John and Fanny's son George Barnard Hankey was baptised in Fetcham on the 27 April 1873 and was quite a local hero on his return from the Boer War in 1900 with a parade in The Street, Fetcham, led by Bookham Brass Band with villagers pulling the carriage. The school log book of 5 July referred to the event as follows: 'Great rejoicing in the village – welcome to Lieut. G B Hankey on his return from the war.   Several children requested to leave early'.

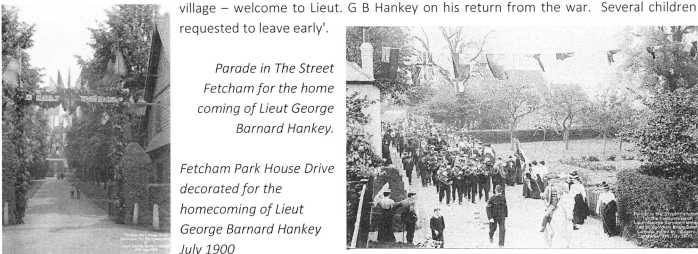

Parade in The Street Fetcham for the home coming of Lieut George Barnard Hankey.

Fetcham Park House Drive decorated for the homecoming of Lieut George Barnard Hankey July 1900

George married Olive B Sturgis on 18 October 1900 at St Michael, Mickleham and during World War One she served as a part time member of the Voluntary Aid Detachment at the Red House Auxillary Hospital in Leatherhead from November 1916 until 1917. *The Surrey Advertiser* of 23 Janaury 1915 carried a report that 'Captain G F B Hankey of Fetcham Park, eldest son of the late Mr J Barnard Hankey, and who is in the King's Royal Rifles, was seriously wounded in action last week. He was taken to a hospital at Boulogne, and this week more favourable reports have been received on his condition'. Dorothea, John's eldest daughter married a stockbroker, Louis Paine in 1896.

EDWARD BARNARD HANKEY was baptised on the 30 May 1875 in Fetcham and married Katharine Elizabeth Dohan in 1908. Hart's Annual Army List 1908 shown him listed with the Worcester Regiment as an Aide de Camp to Admiral Sir F G D Bedford, having been promoted from 2nd Lieutenant to Lieutenant in March 1899 and made Captain in September 1900. The 1911 Census showed Edward and Katharine living Bank House, Whittington, Worcestershire.

Years Ser. Full Pay.	Half Pay.	*The Worcestershire Regiment.* CAPTAINS.	2ND LIEUT.	LIEUT.	CAPTAIN.
13	...	Edwd. Barnard Hankey, *Aide de Camp* to Admiral Sir F. G. D. Bedford......	7 Dec. 95	6 Mar. 99	1 Sept. oo
13	...	4 Henry Astell Lang, Adjutant 23 Nov.04	7 Dec. 95	10 May 99	1 Sept. oo
12	...	Robert A. Cleghorn Linington Leggett....	24 Mar. 97	24 June 99	29 Dec. oo
11	...	1 Gerald Ernest Lea, 6 with rank of Major..	15 May 97	24 June 99	29 Dec. oo
11	...	J. Henry Morris Arden, *Egyptian Army*	15 May 97	22 Oct. 99	29 Dec. oo

Hart's Annual Army List, 1908 for Edward Barnard Hankey

Edward Barnard Hankey Worcestershire Regiment

Edward served with the Worcestershire Regiment throughout the war and the Dorking and Leatherhead Advertiser 9 January 1915 reported *'the casualty list published on Wednesday contained the announcement that Major E B Hankey, Worcestershire Regiment had been wounded in action. In the latter part of November Major Hankey was home on short leave, and up to that time had had some thrilling expericnces with the Worcesters, who have been in the thick of the fighting, Major Hankey being one of the five officers of the regiment left out of sixteen who went out with his regiment. It was satisfactory to learn that Major Hankey's wounds are not regarded as serious, although if the bullet which inflicted the injury had travelled a little farther the prospects of recovery would not have been so rosy.*

Major Hankey is the second son of the late J Barnard Hankey of Fetcham Park. He entered the army from the Militia in December 1895. He was made a captian in 1900 and obtained his majority last March. During the Boer War he saw service in the Orange River Colony, including the action at Wittebergen and in the Transvaal, and was severely wounded. The Queen's Medal, with three clasps was awarded him. From 1902 to 1904 he was employed with the Egyptian Army, and from Arpil 1906 to December 1907 he served as A D C to the Governor of West Austrtalia. His age is 39.'

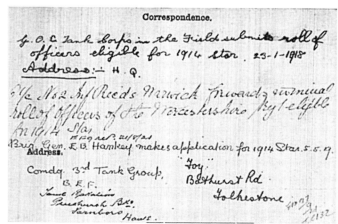

Edward Barnard Hankey Medal Card

The *Dorking and Leatherhead Advertiser* dated 5 January 1918 reported that Lieutenant Colonel E B Hankey, second son of the late Mr J Barnard Hankey of Fetcham Park has been awarded the DSO and had a few weeks earlier presented with the freedom of the City of Worcester in recognition of his gallantry at the battle of Ypres.

Edward died in March 1959 in Cirencester, Gloucestershire.

A newspaper article dated 27 May 1916 stated '*2nd Lieutenant Thomas Barnard Hankey, brother to Edward had been awarded The Albert Medal (1st Class) for three acts of conspious bravery. On October 15th, 1915, Second-Lieutenant Hankey was in charge of a party under instruction of throwing live grenades. A man who was throwing a grenade with a patent Noble lighter became nervous when the lighter went off, and dropped the grenade at his feet. Second-Lieutenant Hankey at once picked up the grenade and threw it out of the trench. There were four men in this section of the trench. On December 4th, 1915, while Second-Lieutenant Hankey was in charge of a party under instruction in throwing live grenades, a man pulled the pin from a grenade and threw the grenade straight into the parapet. Second-Lieutenant Hankey at once picked up the grenade and threw it over the parapet. There were four men in the throwing pit at the time. On December 6th, 1915, Second-Lieutenant Hankey was in charge of a party under instruction in throwing live grenades from a catapult. A live grenade was placed in the pocket of the catapult, the fuse was lighted and the lever released. The grenade, for some reason, was not thrown by the catapult, and fell out of the pocket on to the ground. Second-Lieutenant Hankey, who was standing on the other side of the catapult to that on which the grenade lay, rushed at the grenade, seized it, and threw it away. The fuse was a short, five second fuse, and the grenade exploded on hitting the ground fifteen yards away. There were eight men near the catapult at the time, and ten others not far away*'.

The Surrey Advertiser of 29 May 1916 explained 'that military decorations could not be awarded in the above cases as the acts of gallantry were not performed in the face of the enemy. He had already received the distinctions of the Croix de Chevalier and the Legion of Honour for conspicuous bravery on September 25 1915'.

FRANCIS JAMES BARNARD HANKEY was born in Fetcham in December 1886. He travelled back and forth across the Atlantic, travelling to Quebec in Canada as a young man in May 1906, and is shown on a 'List or Manifest of Alien Passengers for the United States' as a twenty-five-year-old rancher sailing from Liverpool on 30 March 1912 on the British ocean liner RMS *Caronia,* arriving in New York on 8 April 1912.

RMS Caronia was launched in 1904 by Cunard and on 14 April 1912 sent the first ice warning at 09:00 to RMS Titanic reporting 'bergs, growlers and field ice'.

Francis married Anna Norris in 1915 but had first to obtain dispensation from the Roman Catholic Archbishop of Quebec.

'Wedding 19 January 1915 Protestant and Roman Catholic
'On the nineteenth day of January 1915, whereas the Most Reverend Cardinal Louis Nazaire Bégin, Archbishop of Quebec has granted a dispensation from the law of the church which forbids marriage between Francis J B Hankey, a baptised Protestant, son of age of the late John B Hankey and the late Fanny Ellen Pratt-Barlow of Fetcham, Surrey, England in one part, and Annie C Norris, daughter of age of the late John

William Norris and Jitta Behan of Vancouver on the other part, and whereas a dispensation has been granted from all three banns of marriage we the undersigned present having discovered no other impediment to their marriage have received their mutual consent to be united in the bonds of holy matrimony in the presence of Robert Alexander Black and Margaret A Black'.

Francis served as a 2nd Lieutenant and Captain in the 12th Battalion Kent Royal Rifle Corps from 22 July 1915 and as a Major in the Royal Tank Corps during World War One, being awarded the 1915 Star, Victory and British War Medal.

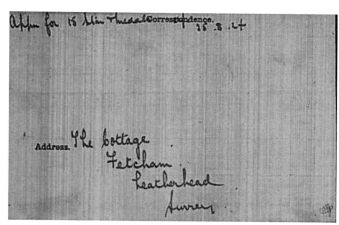

Medal Card for Francis James Barnard Hankey Kent Royal Rifles and Tank Corps

SS Montclare

He returned to England in July 1924 for a holiday and three months later as a thirty-seven-year-old he left London on the SS *Montclare*, built in 1922 for Canadian Pacific Steamships, arriving in Quebec on the 31 October 1924. The 'Declaration of Passenger to Canada' form completed and stamped by Canadian Pacific 62-65 Charing Cross, London SW1 in 1924, stated that he was a Canadian Pacific Railways Employee, returning to Canada on the termination of a vacation and intended to remain permanently in Canada giving an address in Montreal West. It also recorded his port of first arrival in Canada as Quebec May 1906.

The *Ottawa Journal* of 23 February 1942 reported his death as follows: *'Great War Veteran Major Hankey dies. Major Francis James Barnard Hankey, served with the British Imperial Army in France during the First Great War, died in hospital here Saturday. At the time the first war broke out Major Hankey owned large ranches in British Columbia and Alberta'.*

MIRIAM BARNARD HANKEY'S marriage was reported in the Dorking and Leatherhead Advertiser of 5 August 1911 and extracts read *'A wedding which excited unusual interest over a large part of the county of Surrey was solemnised at the Parish Church, Fetcham on Wednesday when Miriam Hankey, youngest daughter of Mr and Mrs J Barnard Hankey was married to Mr Frederick Gordon Dalziel Colman. The bride belongs to a family well known and highly esteemed in the county while in Fetcham and neighbourhood she is held in the warmest regard. The popularity of the bridegroom over a very wide area could hardly be surpassed and during the years he officiated as Master of the Surrey Union Foxhound he not only brought that pack up to a very high standard, but came into close contact with all classes connected with the Hunt. The bride who was given away by her father wore a lovely dress of white brocade, with a train of silver*

tissue. Her ornaments included beautiful diamond earrings, the gift of the bridegroom and a pearl and diamond bracelet, the gift of her mother. The dresses of the bridesmaids were periwinkle blue chiffon over grey satin, and tegal hats with plumes to match. They also wore velvet neck-bands with true lovers' knots in diamonds and carried bouquets of carnations, the gifts of the bridegroom. Mr. Nigel Colman, brother of the bridegroom carried out the duties as Best man.'

An article appeared on 1 December 1917 in the *Illustrated Sporting and Dramatic News* entitled *'Sportswomen at War'* and read *'Mrs Frederick Coleman was a name to conjure with in the days of Richmond Horse Shows, or anywhere else where Shetland ponies were in the ring; just as under her maiden name of Miss Miriam Hankey nobody rode straighter to hounds from their very earliest childhood. Now Mrs Coleman is driving cars for the Royal Flying Corps and sometimes old friends find her sitting waiting in her car somewhere in the Surrey country she knows so well, or driving big lorries through all sorts of troublesome traffic. It is arduous work but necessary, and it is just the sportswomen, used all their lives to open air in all weathers, who are best fitted to replace men in these sort of ways'.*

By contrast in November 1922 the *Dundee Courier* ran the following article: *'An Interesting Wedding - Nullity Suits Recalled. An unusual, if not unique feature of a society wedding which took place in London yesterday afternoon was the fact that both the bride and bridegroom, described in the register as 'spinster' and 'batchelor' respectively, had been married before and had afterwards figured in nullity suits. The bride, Miss Miriam Bernard Hankey, youngest daughter of the late Mr. John Barnard Hankey, Fetcham Park, Surrey and Mrs. Bernard Hankey, The Cottage, Fetcham, was married in 1911 to Mr. Frederick Gordon Dalziel Colman. In May last year, after ten years of married life, Mrs Coleman brought a suit of nullity against her husband. The case is a remarkable one, and created a sensation at the time. It ended in the then Lord Chancellor granting Mrs Colman the decree of nullity asked for. The bridegroom, Captain Guy De Houghton, DSO, MC, King's Own Yorkshire Light Infantry was married to Miss Violet Caroline Townley Parker in 1917 and in 1919 Mrs De Houghton succeeded in a nullity suit which she brought against him. The wedding took place at St Martin's Register Office, Covent Garden. Only four friends were present. The bride wore a brown costume, with hat to match'.*

Nullity of marriage is a declaration by a court that your supposed marriage is null and void, and that no valid marriage exists between you and your partner. In other words, it is a declaration that the supposed marriage never happened. Nullity (or annulment) is not the same as divorce.

Miriam and Guy were divorced in 1938 after 16 years of marriage. She was 46 years old. She married for the third time in the late summer of 1947.

ERNEST OLIVER RUSSELL HINDER

Ernest was born in October 1882 in Wheatenhurst, Gloucestershire, and was an only child. His father Albert was an agricultural labourer. By the age of eighteen Ernest had moved to Fetcham and the 1901 census recorded him working as a Footman to Mr C S Gordon Clark.

Fetcham Lodge

1901 Census Fetcham Lodge

Ernest lived at Fetcham Lodge, although Mr Gordon Clark does not appear to have been resident at the time of the census. The household also included a Butler, a Cook, two Housemaids and a Kitchen maid. The property also had a Coach House where a Groom and a Coachman and his family lived, and a Cottage where the Gravett family lived. Many garden parties were held in the grounds. Ernest remained in the service of Mr Gordon Clark, and finally became the Butler until 1915 when he enlisted as a rifleman with the 16th (County of London) Battalion, Queen's Westminster Rifles, Regimental Number 551774.

Recruits outside The Queen's Westminsters Office September 1914   *Medal Card Ernest Hinder*

Ernest saw service in Egypt, Palestine, Salonika and France and during 1918 Ernest, serving with the 1/16th (County of London) Battalion (Queen's Westminster Rifles) would have taken part in The First Battle of Arras, The Battle of Albert, The Battle of the Scarpe, The Battle of the Canal du Nord, The Battle of the Cambrai, and The Pursuit to the Selle which took place in the last 100 days of the war, when the Allies were chasing the Germans out of France and Belgium back into Germany.

Sadly, he was to die from pneumonia on 26 October at the age of thirty-six, sixteen days before the Armistice was declared. In the spring of 1918

large numbers of soldiers in the trenches in France became ill. The soldiers complained of a sore throat, headaches and a loss of appetite. Although it appeared to be highly infectious, recovery was rapid and doctors gave it the name of 'three-day fever'. At first doctors were unable to identify the illness but eventually they decided it was a new strain of influenza.

For the next few months soldiers continued to be infected with the virus but there were very few fatalities. However, in the summer of 1918, symptoms became much more severe. About a fifth of the victims developed bronchial pneumonia or septicemia blood poisoning. A large percentage of these men died.

By the end of the summer the virus had reached the German Army. The virus created serious problems for the German military leadership as they found it impossible to replace their sick and dying soldiers. The infection had already reached Germany and over 400,000 civilians died of the disease in 1918. The first cases of the influenza epidemic in Britain appeared in Glasgow in May, 1918. It soon spread to other towns and cities and during the next few months the virus killed 228,000 people in Britain. This was the highest mortality rate for any epidemic since the outbreak of cholera in 1849.

Ernest was buried at the Pont-de-Nieppe Communal Cemetery, Departement du Nord, France.

The Pont-De-Nieppe Communal Cemetery was used by Commonwealth field ambulances and fighting units from October 1914 to March 1918, by German troops during the summer of 1918, and by Commonwealth troops again in September-November 1918. The German graves were later removed to the adjoining German cemetery. The cemetery now contains 135 Commonwealth burials of the First World War, 11 of them unidentified.

The Dorking and Leatherhead Advertiser carried an article on the 9 November 1918 which referred to Ernest's death. *'Pte Ernest Hinder of the Queen's Westminsters, died in hospital in France from pneumonia following on from influenza on October 26th. He had been home on leave quite recently, and had only been back in France ten days when he died. Pte Hinder was 36 years of age and was butler to Mr C S Gordon Clark, C.C., when he joined up about three years ago. His home was in Gloucestershire, and he had been in service at Fetcham Lodge about sixteen years. He had seen service in Egypt, Palestine, Salonika and France. Pte Hinder was well known and very popular in Fetcham and Leatherhead, and was for many years a member of the Leatherhead Unionist Club. He was always a member of the Fetcham Choir which competed at the Leith Hill Musical Festival.'*

Probate was granted in London on the 18 December 1918 and Ernest's effects of £410 were left to Charles Stanley Gordon Clark, Esquire. His mother Mary died in December 1918 in Wheatenhurst, and his father Albert passed away in September 1919. His former employer, Mr Gordon Clark was an affluent and prominent member of the Fetcham community and in 1926 he became High Sheriff of Surrey, although sadly Ernest was not to witness this. Mr Gordon Clark also gave five acres of his land to the National Playing Fields Association for a public recreation ground, thus creating Cock Lane Recreation Ground.

Influenza In Surrey – A Widespread Epidemic

During the autumn and winter of 1918 an influenza epidemic was to sweep the world, affecting the fighting men and their friends and families at home alike. The *Surrey Advertiser* of the 28 October ran the following article:

'Influenza in Surrey – A widespread Epidemic

Surrey had not escaped the prevailing epidemic of influenza, and from all parts of the county come reports of schools closed in consequence of the scourge, and of numbers of victims among the people. But, so far as we have been able to gather, there have been comparatively few deaths among the civil population as a result of the epidemic, and if people who are threatened take prompt care of themselves there is no reason for undue alarm.

In the camps, it is a different matter. There influenza has claimed victims by hundreds, and unfortunately a goodly number of cases have had a fatal termination. The military authorities are doing all that is possible with a wholly inadequate medical staff to deal with the situation.

As stated, schools have been or are being closed all over the place. All the elementary schools in Woking have been closed for a week or two, and at Chobham, Byfleet, Ripley, Leatherhead, Kingston, Long Ditton, Malden, Chessington, Guildford, and many other districts it has been deemed advisable to prevent the children from assembling and spreading infection.

Doctors everywhere are extremely hard worked. One at Kingston stated that he had visited no fewer than sixty patients; another at Working said: "From early morning till late at night I have done nothing but rush from one 'flu' patient to another" and almost all medical men could tell the same tale.

At Bookham the only doctor was himself a victim, and at Leatherhead two other medical men were temporarily put hors de combat by the complaint.

Dr Brind, at Chertsey Rural Council on Tuesday, said a good many people who had the "snivels" thought they had influenza, but fortunately for them it was not that complaint.'

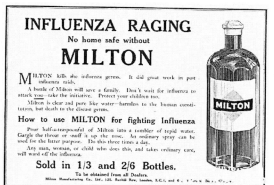
The Sketch Magazine, 1919

Dorking and Leatherhead Advertiser 1918

THE TWO HOCKLEY BROTHERS

In 1901 Charles Hockley, a thirty-seven-year-old Carter on a farm was living with his wife Alice and their family at Silvermere Lodge in Hersham. They had a sixteen-year-old daughter Emily, and five sons fourteen-year-old Charles, a farm worker, eleven-year-old George born in Chertsey, eight-year-old Harry born in Effingham, five-year-old William born in Cobham and two-year-old Sidney born in Hersham. By 1911 the family had moved to Pachesham, Leatherhead and Alice and Charles had been married for twenty-seven years. Charles was employed as a stockman and his eighteen-year-old daughter Emily was a laundress, Harry was a cowman whilst younger brother William worked as a gardener. Thirteen-year-old Sidney was not shown on the census form. George married Edith Dainton in October 1915 at Holy Trinity Church, Westcott. Young Sidney was to have a brush with the law in 1915 when as a seventeen-year-old he was to be caught riding his bicycle without a light. The *Dorking and Leatherhead Advertiser* of 30 January reported his demeanour.

'FETCHAM - NO LIGHT At the Epsom Petty Sessions on Monday, before Mr. B. Braithwaite (Chairman) and other magistrates, Sidney Hockley, Pound Farm, Fetcham was summoned for riding a bicycle without a light in Stoke Road, Fetcham, on January 13th. Defendant pleaded "Guilty". P.C. Lewis said at 8.15pm on the evening in question defendant riding a bicycle without a light. When he spoke to defendant he said his lamp had caught alight and had fallen to pieces. A fine of 5s. was imposed.'

Pound Corner showing Shamrock Cottage circa 1900. This was the farm cottage for Pound Farm. Demolished 1950's

Sidney enlisted when he was eighteen and gave his occupation as an Engineer's Apprentice. He served with the Army Service Corps as a Driver and Fitter.

The entry in the Parish Register for St Matthews, Hatchford showed that although older brother Harry was born in 1893 he wasn't baptised until May 1901.

Harry was to serve in the 12th Bn. King's Royal Rifle Corps Regimental number 14114 entering the theatre of war in France on 28 May 1915. His name too was to appear, more tragically in the local newspaper, this time the Surrey Advertiser dated 8 July 1916.

WOUNDED.

13530 Bombardier J. W. Jones, R.F.A. (Sutton); 3468 Pte. E. Sloan, Royal West Kent Regiment (Ash Green); 14114 Pte. H. J. Hockley, K.R.R.C. (Fetcham), 1486 Lance-Corpl A. Parratt, K.R.R.C. (Ripley); 12213 Pte. H. Wil-

Private H J Hockley KRRC 14114 (Fetcham) Surrey Advertiser 8 July 1916

Harry Hockley's baptism Parish Register for St Matthews

The War Diary for the 12th Battalion King's Royal Rifle Corps for the days from the 1-16 of July referred to the battalion being in Reserve at Ypres on the first of July and then relieving the 12th Rifle Brigade in the Front Line at Potijer on the 2nd. Between the 2-8 July enemy artillery was fairly active against our front line and also about Battalion Headquarters, Potijer Wood which resulted in four fatalities and thirteen wounded, one of them likely to have been Harry. On the 9 July, there is a report of enemy Lachrymatory shells more commonly known as 'tear gas' being fired which would have caused anything from a mild irritation to an intense stinging sensation according to the concentration, followed by profuse watering of the eyes and spasm of the eyelids making it impossible to keep the eyes open. With a rise in the concentration of the vapour, further effects of the gas on the respiratory passages and lungs produced a burning feeling in the throat and discomfort in the chest, nausea and vomiting. The gas was intended to incapacitate opposing soldiers rather than to kill.

WAR DIARY July 1916 12 KRRC Vol 12 CONFIDENTIAL			
	Date	*Hour*	*Summary of Events and Information*
YPRES	1st		In Reserve at YPRES
"	2nd		Relieved 12th RIFLE BRIGADE in Front Line etc., at POTIJER. Map Sheet 28, 1/10,000
"	2-8		In Front Line at POTIJER. Enemy artillery fairly active against our front line and also about Battalion Headquarters, POTIJER WOOD (7th). Casualties – 4 O.R. Killed, 13 wounded.
"	9th		Relieved by 12th RIFLE BRIGADE and proceeded to billets in YPRES. Batt. H.Q. – CONVENT.
"	9-10		In Reserve at YPRES. During this period enemy shelled the town fairly heavily, using *lachrymatory shells.

"	10th.		Relieved by 12th KING'S (61st Brigade) and proceeded to billets in POPERINGHE
POPERINGHE	10-11		In Divisional Reserve at POPERINGHE
"	12th	10p m.	Owing to enemy shelling POPERINGHE, orders were received to evacuate the town, and Battalion marched to 'J' Camp, outside POPERINGHE, Sheet 28. Casualties, - 3 O.R. Killed, 2 wounded.
"	13th		At 'J' Camp.
ERQUINGHEM	116th	9pm.	Marched to billets at FLEURBAIX, Disposition of Batt., Headquarters, MARE'S NEST, Rue de Blanche, A COY. SCHOOL, RUE DE GUESNE. B COY. FERRETS POST. C COY. JAY POST, CITY POST, HUDSON BAY. D COY, ELBOW FARM, CHAPEL FARM.

Transcription from the original War Diary King's Royal Rifle Corps July 1916

Throughout the war Poperinge, or "Pops" as the British soldiers called it, was used by the British Army as a gateway to the battlefields of the northern Ypres Salient. It was an important rail centre behind the front line and was used for the distribution of supplies, for billeting troops, for casualty clearing stations and for troops at rest from duty in the forward trench areas. Thousands of troops passed through this small town which was frequently targeted by long range German artillery. During the Third Battle of Ypres (31 July to 10 November 1917) Poperinge and the surrounding area was bombed by German aircraft with some bombs landing on the Casualty Clearing Stations nearby.

British troops on London buses Poperinghe (original spelling)

Four months after the report of Harry's wounding he married Emily Friday at St Mary's Church, Fetcham in November 1916. He was twenty-four and was shown as a Lance Corporal in HM Army. Emily, the daughter of James Friday, a Gas Stocker was born in Dorking in August 1889 and was three years older than Harry. Her address on the marriage certificate is shown as Leatherhead

Harry's medal card showed that he was transferred to the Labour Corps, Regimental number 245322. He was awarded the Victory, British Medal and the 1915 Star as well as the Silver War Medal awarded to injured servicemen. He was discharged early in 1918.

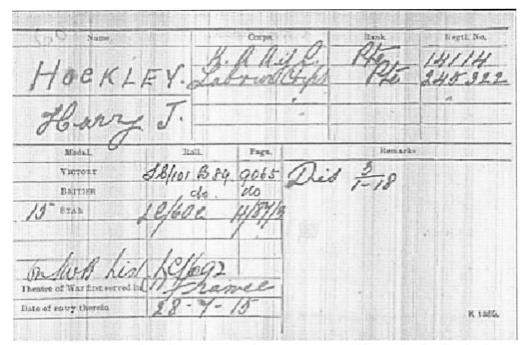

Emily Friday

Harry J Hockley Medal Card

Eldest brother Charles had married Eliza Winters at the Parish Church in Cobham in 1904 and when he enlisted in 1917 as a thirty-one-year-old he and wife Eliza had two daughters Ivy and May and were living at 1 Camden Cottages, Church Walk, Weybridge Charles served with the Royal Engineers, Railway Construction Company.

After the war the Electoral Roll for 1920 showed Emily and Harry, together with his brothers Sidney and William living at Moor Cottages in Fetcham.

EDWARD IRELAND

Edward George Ireland was baptised in St Mary's Church, Fetcham on the 24 April 1892. He was the son of Jacob, a plate layer born in Ewhurst and Alice. The 1911 showed the family living at 25 Kingslea, Kingston Road, Leatherhead and Edward was a nineteen-year-old Groom, with two younger sisters Florence born in 1895 and Violet in 1898.

He was to attest as an eighteen-year-old on 4 September 1911 at Kingston on Thames and entered the theatre of war on the 20 August 1914. He served with the Royal Army Medical Corps. Regimental number 5708, and 5th Reserve Park Army Service Corps. Army records described him as five feet six inches tall, with a fresh complexion, brown eyes and hair. He weighed 110 lbs.

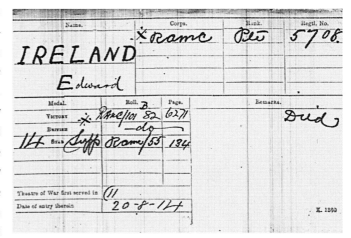

Edward Ireland's Medal Card

Royal Army Medical Corps postcard

Edward died at the No. 10 Stationary Hospital in St Omer on 22 January 1915. He was twenty-two old. The Base Hospital was part of the casualty evacuation chain, further back from the front line than the Casualty Clearing Stations. They were manned by troops of the Royal Army Medical Corps, with attached Royal Engineers and men of the Army Service Corps. In the theatre of war in France and Flanders, the British hospitals were generally located near the coast. They needed to be close to a railway line, in order for casualties to arrive (although some also came by canal barge); they also needed to be near a port where men could be evacuated for longer-term treatment in Britain.

There were two types of Base Hospital, known as Stationary and General Hospitals. They were large facilities, often centred on some pre-war buildings such as seaside hotels. The hospitals grew hugely in number and scale throughout the war. Most of the hospitals moved very rarely until the larger movements of the armies in 1918. Some hospitals moved into the Rhine bridgehead in Germany and many were operating in France well into 1919. Most hospitals were assisted by voluntary organisations, most notably the British Red Cross.

Edward is remembered at Longuenesse Souvenir Cemetery

No.10 Stationary Hospital in St Omer

FREDERICK CHARLES JOHNSON – A Promise Fulfilled and a Poignant Letter

Frederick Johnson was born in Westminster in 1883, and was one of nine children. His father John was a Railway Porter born in Berkshire. The 1901 census showed that seventeen-year-old Frederick also became a Porter with the railways like his father. Some seven years later on the 7 June 1908, he married Rose May Hoare in West Horsley. He was twenty-five and she was twenty-two years old. Rose's mother was incidentally born in Westminster.

Frederick became a postman and in 1911 lived at The Street, West Horsley with wife Rose and their two-year-old son Harold. Later he was attached to Leatherhead Post Office and the Electoral Rolls for the years 1913, 1914 & 1915 showed Frederick as a tenant living in Cobham Road, Fetcham.

Frederick enlisted in the 1st Battalion, East Surrey Regiment. Service No. Pte L/8253. His medal roll card shows he entered the Theatre of War on 11 September 1914.

Frederick's son Kenneth was baptised in St Mary's Church, Fetcham on the 31 January 1915. The entry in the Parish records described Frederick as a 'Postman – now on King's Service'.

Entry in St Mary's Church Parish Records January 1915

Three months later he was killed in action and died on the 27 April 1915.   The following diary extract is taken from The Queen's Royal Surrey Regimental Association East Surrey War Diaries and is dedicated to the 8,000 men of the Queen's Royal Regiment (West Surrey) and 6,000 men of the East Surrey Regiment, many of whose bodies lie in Flanders.

TRENCHES SOUTH OF YPRES

26th April 1915	A fine day. Trenches shelled by light field gun and trench mortar intermittently. Total Casualties: 2 other ranks killed and 1 wounded.
27th.	Fine sunny day. Shelling a little more quiet. Total casualties: 1 other ranks killed and 12 wounded..
28th.	Fine sunny day, usual shelling. Total casualties: 7 other ranks wounded.
29th.	Still fine. trenches on BLUFF and about it shelled with light field guns and trench mortar from 2 a.m. to 2 p.m. Total casualties 2 other ranks killed and 3. wounded. 2 Lts. R. B. Unwin, R. W. Burton & A. F. Topley joined Battn. today
30th.	Fine sunny weather. A quiet day. Relieved by Manchester's during night and marched back to bivouac near KRUISSTRAAT Captain E. M. Woulfe-Flanagan, 2nd Lt. J.C. Druce & H. M. Caffyn and Lt. G. Saunders 4th Bn. Joined the Battn. today, with 300 other ranks. Total Casualties 2 other ranks killed & 3 wounded

Transcription of the letter from Brigadier General F S Maude

My dear Darwell

I had a letter last night from Sir Chas Ferguson giving me an outline of the operations around Hill 60 in the course of which he says that the East Surreys and the Bedfords were "the heroes of the occasion" and again "you may well be proud of your East Surreys", whose conduct was "magnificent". I have also this morning seen an officer of the Norfolks who was wounded in the vicinity of Hill 60 and he tells me that he has never been so proud of belonging to the British Army as he is now after witnessing all that happened in the fighting last week, and the grim determination and tenacity of all our troops, especially the East Surreys.

Sir Charles did not give me many details, but he mentioned that Paterson had been killed and that you were comdg. the Battn. also that you have had from 300 to 400 casualties. I see in the papers too that Wynyard is among the killed.

Meagre though the above details are they are sufficient to show me that your splendid regiment has ones more added to its imperishable renown and no doubt when the story of the fight comes to be more fully written we shall realize more and more how the Army and the Country are indebted to your glorious men for their indomitable courage and grit.

For myself I cannot tell you how proud I am of you all. Since I have had the honour of commanding this splendid Brigade the East Surreys hare earned from me nothing but the highest commendation for their work whether in the field and in quarters, and, knowing you as I do, it is Just what I expected of you all. My only regret is that I was not able to meet you as you came off the Hill and tell the men how filled with admiration we all are at their splendid conduct, but I hope, if all goes well to start back in a weeks time and see you all before very long.

I am afraid that the casualties hare been very heavy. The loss of Paterson and Wynyard will, I know. be greatly felt in the Regiment, to me they are an irreparable loss, and I dread looking at the papers for fear that I shall find the names of some of the gallant young officers who have done such grand work during the past six months.

May the imperishable glory of your great deeds stand forth, as I know they will, as a brilliant example to those who will hereafter have the privilege of joining the ranks of your fine old regiment.

My sincerest sympathy with all the wounded In their sufferings and best love to you all.

Yours very sincerely,

F, S, MAUDE

G, HYSON, Lieut, for Captain,

Comdg, 1ˢᵗ Bn, East Surrey Regt

> 'They went with songs to the battle, they were young,
> Straight of limb, true of eye, steady and aglow
> They were staunch to the end against odds uncounted
> They fell with their face to the foe.
> They mingle not with their laughing comrades again
> They sit no more at familiar tables of home
> They have no lot in our labour of the day time
> They sleep beyond England's foam'.

Frederick is remembered at CWD Grave ID13 Chester Farm Cemetery, Belgium. He was posthumously awarded the Victory and British Medals, 1914 Star and Clasp.

Chester Farm Cemetery, Belgium

An article in the Surrey Advertiser dated 22 May 1915 referred to his death. Mrs Johnson had had no news of her husband for upwards of a month when she received a letter from Private H J Mustoe of the 1st East Surrey which was forwarded onto her by Mr Friston, the sub-postmaster at Fetcham. She had had no official confirmation of her husband's death.

'Although not officially confirmed it appears that Pte. F.C. Johnson of the 1st East Surrey, was killed in action on 27th April. Pte. Johnson was a reservist and had been a postman attached to Leatherhead Post Office. He was called up at the outbreak of the war and went out to the front soon afterwards with his regiment.

Mrs Johnson resides at Fetcham with her two children, and has had no news of her husband for upwards of a month when details of his death were conveyed to her in the following letter, sent to Mr. Friston, sub-postmaster at Fetcham, on Tuesday, by Pte. H J Mustoe of the 1st East Surrey, who is at present in hospital at Whalley, near Blackburn:-

'Just a line to ask you to offer Mrs Johnson very great regret for the grief caused by the death of her husband. He was a postman at Fetcham and my comrade in my section, and we promised to write to each other's people in case anything happened to either of us. Will you tell her I was with him in his last moments and closed his eyes when death took place. He was a nice quite chap and was well liked throughout the platoon – we always used to share our bit of grub and the blanket together. I don't know the proper address, but will you kindly tell his wife, and tell her he died like a true Britisher and a soldier. He was killed on April 27th, and I carried him out of the trench, and, funny to relate, I got wounded myself just after. I only gave him a letter from home about an hour before and he seemed so pleased. The talk we used to have about my coming down to see him – I belong to Putney, S.W. – when the war was over. But God's will be done; and tell her I hope time will soften the blow. But I expect the War Office has sent long before now, that's what I have been waiting for.'

Frederick is also remembered with honour on the War Memorial at St Mary's Church.

ALFRED WOOLDRIDGE MEDD – The Cap Badge and the Missing Link

The Well House stands in the Old Street, Fetcham. It was formerly known as Laburnum Cottage and is believed to be late 17th Century. The house has many lovely old features and various artefacts have been found around the house and gardens by its owners, such as old bottles, a small jar, a cigarette packet, clay pipes and a regimental cap badge. These were interesting but not remarkable, however on further examination they slowly revealed a family connection to one of the men who died in World War One, Alfred Medd.

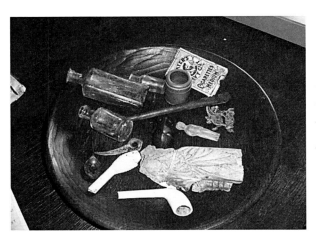

Display of artefacts found – courtesy of present owner

Laburnum Cottage, 1940

99

Alfred Wooldridge Medd was born on the 26 November 1880 and was baptised on Christmas Day in North Cerney, Gloucestershire. The 1881 Census showed his father Peter Goldsmith Medd as a 51-year-old priest who lived with his wife Louisa (nee Nesbit) and their three children, Frederick, Alan and Alfred at North Cerney Rectory. The household also included a nurse domestic servant, a housemaid and a cook.

Alfred Medd as a young man

By 1911 Alfred was thirty years old and lived with his sixty-two-year-old widowed mother Louisa, and his brother Frederick, a' Russia Merchant', and younger siblings Mary and Henry. No occupation was recorded for Alfred. The family lived at 45 The Vineyards, Abingdon, Berkshire and had four servants.

On 7 January 1913 Alfred married thirty-year-old Hilda Maud Scholes at Christ Church, St Marylebone, Westminster. His rank or Profession was described as 'Gentleman.'

The Marriage Register Christ Church St. Marylebone

Initial research of Alfred's military service during World War One and his Medal Card, indicated he had served with The Queen's Royal West Surrey Regiment, as a Private, Regimental number G/24895 and was awarded the Victory and British Medal.

During the conflict, Alfred and Hilda were to have two sons, Peter born in September 1915 in Marylebone and David in 1917. Sadly, Alfred was to lose his life on 5 September 1918 and his name is one of those engraved on the Fetcham War Memorial.

Alfred Medd in military uniform

The Fetcham War Memorial

Alfred is also remembered at Grootebeek British Cemetery in Belgium. The memorial gives the following information:

'Alfred Woodridge Medd, the son of Peter Goldsmith Medd (Priest), North Cerney, Glos. Husband of Hilda Medd of 2A Oxford and Cambridge Mansions, London. Date of Death 5 September 1918 aged 37. Regiment The Queen's (Royal West Surrey), 10th battalion. Service number 24895.'

Alfred Medd headstone Grootebeek British Cemetery Belgium

Grootebeek British Cemetery Belgium

The Cheltenham Chronicle dated 5 October 1918 reported his death as follow:

'KILLED IN ACTION Lance-Corpl. Alfred Wooldridge Medd, R.W. Surrey Regiment, killed in action on Sept. 5, was the third son of the late Rev. Canon Peter Goldsmith Medd (for about 40 years rector of North Cerney, near Cirencester and of Mrs. Medd, of Fetcham, Surrey. He was 37 years of age.'

10th QUEENS R.W.S.REGT.

SHEET 28 1/40.000 KEMMEL

1/2	Battn in Front Line. Relieved by 7th Bn Cheshire Regt 102nd Infy Bde and fell back into Reserve Area (OUDERDOM) Battn H.Q. situated G.24.b.5.8.

DICKEBUSCH

2/3	Battn Relieved 3rd Bn 105th Infy Regt. 27th American Division in Front Line (DICKENBUSCH SECTOR)
3rd	Battn in Line. Dispositions unaltered.
4th	Battn attacked enemy at 5.30a.m. Casualties suffered by Battn in this attack were 1 Off.12 OR. Killed, 2 Offs 24 O.Rks wounded

Night

5/6th	Battn relieved by COY of 10th R W Kent's and 2Coys of the 26th Fusiliers in the front line and fell back into reserve at OUDERDOM.Occupied same billets as night 1/2nd inst.

Transcribe as written from the original Diaries

Source: Queens Regiment Museum

The War Diary for 10th Queen's Royal West Surrey Regiment describing the Regiment's movements at the time of Alfred's death

The 1919 Electoral Roll revealed Alfred's widow Hilda and his children Peter and David lived at Laburnum Cottage in The Street, Fetcham. His mother and brother Henry had also moved to Fetcham and were shown in residence at Sunnyside, a property close to The Bell PH. It is unclear as to when the families had relocated here. There appeared to be no connection to the regimental cap badge found in the property. The Medd family had lived there – Alfred Medd had been a fatality of WW1 – but from the initial records found it was believed he had served in The Queen's Royal West Surrey Regiment. The cap badge found was that of The Buffs.

Alfred's Mother Louisa

The *De Ruvigny's Roll of Honour 1914-1918* lists the following entry:

'MEDD ALFRED WOOLDRIDGE Lance Corp. No. 24895 10th (Service) battn. Queen's (Royal West Surrey) Regn. 3rd son of the late Rev. Canon Peter Goldsmith Medd, by his wife, Louisa (Sunnyside, Fetcham) nee Nesbitt. born. North Cerney 26 Nov. 1880. Educ. Winchfield; Marlborough and Keble College, Oxford: was in business: joined the Buffs in May 1916, served with the Expeditionary Force in France and Flanders, also in Italy from Sept. 1917; transferred to the Queen's (Royal West Surrey) Regt. on arrival in France and was killed in action at Ouderdon 5 Sept. 1918. Buried there. He married at Christ Church, Marylebone, London. 7th Jan. 1913. Hilda Maud (2A Oxford and Cambridge Mansions, London N.W.) dau. of Charles Robert Scholes of Dewsbury co. York, Solicitor. Had two sons, Peter Goldsmith b. 18 July 1915 and Stephen Robert Alfred b. 26 July 1916.'

This now provided the missing link– Alfred had indeed served with the Queen's (Royal West Surrey) Regiment and had died whilst with the regiment, but he had originally joined the Buffs in May 1916

– the cap badge had led to uncovering the full story of his military service and sacrifice.

The Buffs Cap Badge (found in Laburnham Cottage).

ARTHUR MOORE – Corn Miller and Business Man

Arthur Moore was born in Leatherhead in 1867 and was the son of Elizabeth Ann and Henry Moore, a corn and coal merchant. The 1891 census showed Arthur living with his parents and two sisters at Gothic Lodge in Leatherhead High Street, where they had two servants, a cook and a housemaid. Arthur's occupation was given as an 'Assistant Wool Stapler', grading fleeces and making the wool ready for spinning and weaving. He married Kate Octavia Slade in 1893. Following the death of the Fetcham Miller, his father Henry added milling to his business and from 1895 when Arthur joined him, traded as Henry Moore & Son retailing corn, flour, seed, hay, straw, meal and artificial manure. By 1901 Arthur and Kate were living at Highlands, in Clinton Road, Leatherhead and Arthur now described himself as a 'Corn and Coal Merchant and Miller'.

His father Henry moved to Fetcham Mill House in 1903 and upon his death in 1915 Arthur took up residence where he remained throughout the war year. Although there was a fire in 1917 and the Mill was destroyed, the Mill House escaped serious damage.

Mill Pond

Arthur's business diversity was illustrated in the local newspapers, such as the advertisement in April 1914 for the sale by auction of his pedigree cows, heifers and bulls or in 1915 for Chicken Powder, 'containing ground insects, but no irritants' sold at 2d a packet.

When the Leatherhead War Agricultural Committee met in June 1917 to discuss the proposal of laying on water to various war time allotments with the Water Company fixing a standpipe at each for the sum of three shilling, Arthur consented to undertake the spraying of potatoes on each allotment at the charge of two pence a rod provided the water was found by the allotment holder.

On 6 July 1918 the *Dorking and Leatherhead Advertiser* carried a report on the theft of corn. Arthur has received an anonymous letter which had prompted him to make enquiries and the Police Court in Epsom charged the miller's assistant who lived at Moore's Cottages, Fetcham and a carman of Gravel Hill, Leatherhead with stealing a sack of unmixed corn of the value of £2 14s. Both men had been in Arthur's employ although another Fetcham resident from River Lane was thought to be the instigator in the case and was charged with receiving the corn well knowing it had been stolen. He received a fine of £3 with the other men receiving a fine of £2 and £1 respectively.

Arthur ran into trouble himself that autumn over his sale of milk and was summoned for offences against the Milk Order. The case was reported in the local press as follow: *'At Epsom on Monday Arthur H Moore cowkeeper and miller, Fetcham was summoned for offences against the Milk Order. There were twenty-one summonses altogether. Frank Augustus Prately, Inspector to the Food Control Committee for the Epsom Rural District, said on 16 August he visited the Mill and interviewed the Carman, who informed him Mr Moore had commenced selling milk by retail in May. In July, it was sold at 7d. a quart, and in August at 9d. a quart. Witness saw Mr Moore, who told him that he did not know it was necessary to be registered.*

By Mr MacMahon: He did not suggest there was any intention of dishonesty on the part of Mr Moore, who allowed him to see his books, and willingly went before the Food Control Committee to explain how the error occurred. Defendant apparently relied upon a general order as to the price of milk, but the local committee had power to vary the price and they did so in August.

Mr Moore said he had kept a herd of cows since 1904 and up to the end of April this year he disposed of all his milk to a local dairyman. The milk being of better quality than other milk he was able to get a better price for it before the prices were fixed. Since the fixing of the prices he had sold it at a loss. In May, he recommended selling the milk by retail, and had not the slightest knowledge that he would have to be registered. He sold the milk according to the prices laid down by the Board of Agriculture Journal. The overcharge was entirely unintentional and since it was pointed out to him he had returned the over-charge to his customers. Mr MacMahon said that his client, although he had committed the offence, had acted quite in ignorance of the law. Defendant was fined £2 for failing to registered as a retailer, £5 for dealing with milk by retail without being registered, and £15 for selling milk above the fixed price'.

Arthur moved to a new house 'Chy Vean' in Oxshott Road in 1920 and bought a plot of land in Kingslea, Leatherhead with corn stores, chaff cutting store, stabling, motor garage and workshop, sack store and a mill and various other buildings. He became a director of the Swan Brewery in Leatherhead and listed in Kelly's 1925 Directory as 'a pig breeder'. When Arthur died in 1934 his company Henry Moore & Son was made into a limited company and the first Managing Director was Redvers Ansell. His estate was left of his widow Kate and Leonard Moritz, a chartered accountant. It amounted to over £2,000,000 in today's money.

FREDERICK ERNEST NELSON

Frederick was born on 18 January 1900 and baptised on 2 March in St Mary's Church, Battersea and was the son Elizabeth (nee Hodder) and Frederick, a Stoker, Petty Officer, in the Royal Navy. The couple's address at the time of his baptism was given as 5 Goulden Street. In 1911 Frederick and his parents and a younger brother Ernest and sister Jessie lived at 3 Mayfield Terrace, Rosebery Road, Epsom. His mother died in January 1914 and by 1917 the family had moved to 1 Stoke Road, Fetcham.

Frederick enlisted on the 12 June 1917 at Guildford and served with the East Surrey Rifles Regimental Number 204453. He gave his age as eighteen although in fact he was only seventeen and a half at that time. He was described as a Butcher's assistant, five feet five inches tall, and unmarried. He had a 'slight spinal curvature' which it was noted 'should disappear with drilling etc.' He was subsequently transferred to the Scottish Rifles on the 27 June 1917 and also served with the Machine Gun Corps Regimental Number 204453.

Military discipline did not sit well with Frederick and his record card had very many misconduct entries which resulted in him being confined to barracks or losing pay. In September 1917, he was confined to barracks (CB) for eight days for 'not complying with an order in that he did not fall in with mess orders when ordered to do so'. He was also 'absent from 08.15 parade' resulting in seven days CB, in December he was late for afternoon Parade with a punishment of three days CB. 1918 did not prove any easier for him starting in January when he was again in trouble for 'leaving Barracks whilst on Picquet' - another seven days CB. 'Fifteen minutes late for parade' – seven days CB, 'Breaking out of barracks after Tattoo. Roll call and returning at 10.30pm' – seven days loss of pay. March brought two more offences – 'Not complying with an order' and 'Late of Parade', this time costing him collectively eighteen days' pay. He was '12 minutes late for his breakfast' in April and was confined to barracks for one day. This pattern continued through the summer months with Frederick 'failing to bathe in the sea when ordered to do so', (seven days CB) 'absent from church parade' (ten days CB), 'Irregular conduct on Parade' (five days CB). At Belton Park, home of the Machine Gun Corps he ran into trouble in October 1918 'absenting himself off parade without permission' and received two hours pack drill as a punishment.

Frederick Nelson's Military Misconduct record

On 7 July 1921 Frederick boarded the P & O steamer 'Borda' and set sail for Adelaide, Australia, accompanied by his father, who had remarried and his brothers and sisters.

761	Nelson Frederick James	The Cottage			Mechanic	45				1				do
	do Ernest	Fetcham Common,					16			1				do
762	do Caroline	Leatherhead			Wife	40				1				do
	do Jessie							15		1				do
	do Vera								7	1				do

Passenger List for Frederick Nelson's family.

P & O Steamship 'Borda'

The 'Borda' made its maiden voyage in March 1914 via the Cape to Australia. During World War 1 it was used as a troopship and in 1920 resumed P & O service to Australia via the Cape.

On 10 July 1923 Frederick married Ada Onley in Holy Trinity Church, Adelaide and in 1930 their son Lisle was born in Large

Bay, Australia. His father died in 1955 and his wife in 1976. Frederick himself passed away in August 1981 all in Ringwood East, Victoria, Australia.

ARTHUR CHARLES PARKER

Arthur was baptised on the 10 October 1880 in St John, Capel, and was the son of James and Catherine Parker who lived in Vicarage Lane. Sadly, his mother died when he was nearly four years old and was buried on 2 July 1884. The 1891 census showed him living with his widowed father James, a general labourer and siblings Jessie, John, Frank, Frederick and Kate.

A transcription of the British Army Service Records 'burnt documents' showed that in 1897 at the age of 18 Arthur joined the 3rd, 2nd Battalion East Surrey Regiment Regimental Number 5236. He was described as 5 feet three inches tall, with fresh complexion, blue eyes and brown hair.

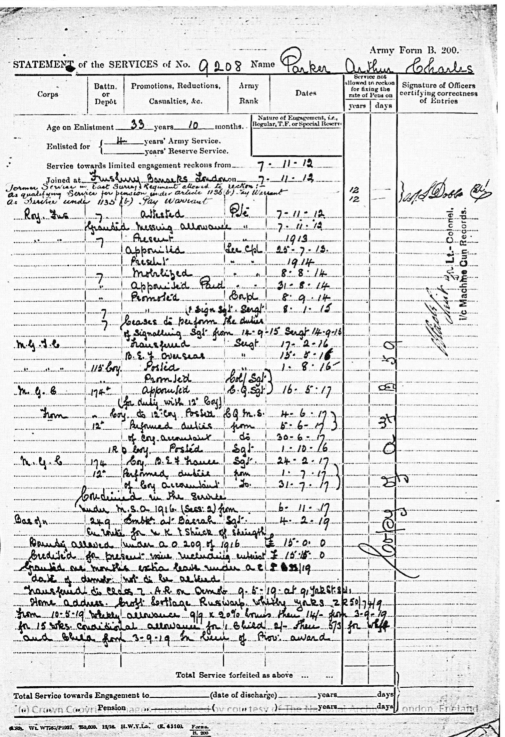

In 1908, he married Laura Atkins and by 1911 the couple were living in Fetcham, at an address shown as Brickfields. Arthur was employed as a domestic gardener and they had a two-year-old daughter Phyllis. On 7 November 1912 at Finsbury he enlisted for four years to serve in the 7th Battalion Royal Fusiliers, Regimental Number 7873. He was appointed Lance Corporal on the 25 July 1913 and promoted to Corporal on 8 September 1914. He was transferred to the Machine Gun Corps on 17 February 1916 holding the rank of Sergeant. His Regimental Number was 9208. He was part of the British Expeditionary Forces and went overseas on 15 May 1916 being promoted to Colour Sergeant in August of that year.

Arthur Parker's Statement of Services

HARRY REEVES

Harry Reeves was born in Chelsea on 23 May 1872 and was the son of Emily and Arthur Reeves, an Engineer Planner. His elder sister Florence was born in 1870 but died as a seven-year-old but he had six other younger brothers and sisters. By 1891 Harry was nineteen and living in Kensington where he was employed as a Footman, Domestic Servant to Julian Leverson, a Major in the Royal Engineers. He married Margaret Morris in October 1899 in St George's Church, Hanover Square, London.

Two years later, the 1901 Census showed Harry at Millfield, Great Bookham, where he was employed as a Manservant to Henry Hansard, Printer to the House of Commons. Harry and Margaret's son Frances was born in Snodland, Kent in 1903 whilst their daughter Mary was born two years later in Kilgerran, Pembrokeshire. In November 1906, their daughter Gwladys was born in Fetcham and the Electoral Roll of 1908 indicated that the family lived at Mark Oak, Fetcham. Muriel, another child was born locally in January 1909, by which time Harry had risen to become a Butler. The children attended Fetcham Village School.

Military records dated 1918 indicated that Harry enlisted at Guildford at the age of forty-six and served with the Duke of Cambridge Own (32nd Middlesex) Football Battalion, Regimental Number 944401, although he did not go overseas.

Harry's wife Margaret died in September 1942 in Fetcham and Harry died on 19 November 1949.

FREDERICK SAINSBURY

Frederick was born in Westing, Wiltshire in 1876 and married Maria Cooper on 28 January 1899 in St Mary's Church, Fetcham. His occupation was described as a Groom and he was twenty-three years old.

In 1911, he and Maria lived at River Lane in Fetcham with their three children, Dorothy aged ten, Francis aged 4 and Louisa who was one year old. He was employed as a Stableman at a Brewery. He enlisted on 24 June 1916 and was called up for service on 16 May 1917. He was now in his early forties and gave his occupation as a Machine Hand, with three children, Francis, Louisa and Harold. He served for 207 days with the Labour Corps, Regimental Number 180887, but was discharged on 8 December 1917 under para 392 XVI King's Regulations as 'No longer physically fit for war service'. His disability was recorded as 'Old thrombosis of veins not due to military service'. His character was described as 'Good'.

He returned home to River Lane and died in 1945 in Fetcham aged seventy, his wife Maria died the following year.

ERNEST GEORGE SAUNDERS

Ernest was baptised in St Mary's Church Fetcham in March 1895, his parents being Emily and Edward, a Carter on a farm. In 1901, the family lived in Stoke Road, Fetcham. In 1911 Ernest, an under gardener, was living at Well Bottom Cottages, Givons Grove, Leatherhead, the home of his Uncle John and his family.

Ernest enlisted at Kingston on 2 September 1914 and was assigned to the East Surrey Regiment, Regimental number 857. He was nineteen years old, five feet two inches tall and weighed 120 lbs. He had blue eyes, a fresh complexion and brown hair. He was sent to France on 1 June 1915.

In 1924, he married May Childs at Twickenham Parish Church. He was twenty-nine and his bride was thirty-six.

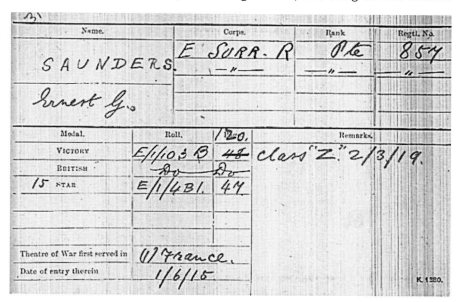

Medal Card for Ernest G Saunders

GEORGE EDWARD WEST

George was baptised in St Mary's Church, Fetcham on 29 January 1888 and was the son of Mary Jane and William West. In 1901, he lived in Great Bookham but by the census of 1911 the family had moved to Ivydene Cottages, Westcroft Road, Wallington Corner. His father William was now sixty-two and a farm labourer and Mary was ten years younger. The household included Alfred and William, both labourers, George himself, now a grocer's assistant, and younger siblings Mabel, Rosina, Arthur and Mary Jane West.

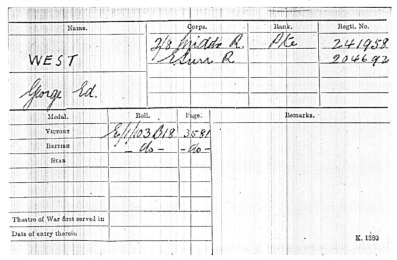

On 12 June 1915 George enlisted with the East Surrey Regiment, Regimental Number 204692 at Wallington. He was twenty-five and five feet six inches tall. He also served with the Middlesex Regiment, Regimental Number 241958.

Medal Card for George West

JAMES HARLOW WHITEN – Life in the Navy

James Harlow Whiten was the son of William and Ada and was born in November 1897 in Fetcham and baptised on 16 January 1898 at St Mary's Church. His father was a coachman and the family lived in Rectory Cottages in 1901 but had moved to Ballards Hall Cottages by 1911. James was thirteen at the time and an only child although his seven-year-old cousin Ada lived with the family.

Records showed that James enlisted in the Navy on 3 April 1915, and gave his occupation as a plumber's mate. He was 5'5" tall with brown hair and blue eyes with a fresh complexion. His service number was J37675 and the first ship he was to serve on HMS *Vivid 1*.

Rectory Cottages, The Street, Fetcham

James Harlow Whitten naval record for World War One

James went on to serve on HMS *Victory 1* from late November 1915 until January 1916, before being transferred to HMS *Malaya* from late January to mid-February 1916. HMS *Malaya* was a Queen Elizabeth-class battleship built for the Royal Navy during the early 1910s. Shortly after commissioning in 1916, she participated in the Battle of Jutland as part of the Grand Fleet. He was to return to HMS *Victory 1* until early May 1916, before being posted to HMS *Bristol*, a light cruiser, where he served until 1919. HMS *Bristol* was in the Adriatic during 1916-17 before going back to South American waters in 1918. She was involved in the 1917 Battle of the Strait of Otranto which was the result of an Austro-Hungarian raid on the Otranto Barrage, an Allied naval blockade of the Strait of Otranto. The battle took place on 14–15 May 1917, and was the largest surface action in the Adriatic Sea during World War I. The Otranto Barrage was a fixed barrier, composed of lightly armed drifters with anti-submarine nets coupled with minefields and supported by Allied naval patrols. The Austro-Hungarian Navy planned to raid the Otranto Barrage in an attempt to break the barrier to allow U-boats freer access to the Mediterranean, and Allied shipping.

HMS *Bristol 1910*

At the end of World War One James was awarded both the Victory Medal and the British War Medal. He married Selina Polhill in Portsmouth in 1911 and their daughter Joyce was born in May 1924. He continued with his naval career and his records show he served on HMS *Gibraltar*, HMS *Columbine*, HMS *Weymouth* and HMS *Despatch*.

In the 1920's he served on HMS *Vernon* which during the First World War, had concentrated on torpedo trials and training and the research and development of anti-submarine devices, mines and ship's electrics. On 1 October 1923, HMS *Vernon* (or *The Vernon* as it came to be known) was established ashore at Portsmouth on the site of the old Gunwharf (now the development known as Gunwharf Quays) and Mining, Whitehead [Torpedo] and Electrical departments were formed.

HMS *Weymouth*

His son Ivan was born in January 1930 although unfortunately he did not live to adulthood and died in 1942 at the age of twelve. James received the RN Long Service and Good Conduct Medal, which referred to Service between 1930 and 1935 serving on HMS *Emperor of India*. In 1931 HMS *Emperor of India* together with HMS *Marlborough* underwent a series of weapons tests that proved to be highly beneficial for future British battleship designs.

James served in World War Two (1942-1945) and was awarded the British Empire Medal and the Distinguished Service Medal (DSM). James himself died in Hythe in 1967 at the age of sixty-nine and was described as a Leading Seaman (Retired).

HMS *Emperor of India*

ARTHUR HAMILTON WINTHROP WOODRUFF

Arthur was the eldest son of the Reverend Arthur William Woodruff and Emily (nee Montague) a British subject who was born in St Petersburg, Russia. He was baptised in Fetcham on 14 February 1888, when the Parish Records showed his father's occupation as 'Clerk in Holy Orders'. In 1891, the family were living in South Stoneham near Southampton where his father was Curate of St Mary's Church. By 1901 Arthur was living with his clergyman father in Walberswick in Suffolk with his nine-year-old brother Keith and four-year-old sister Joan who had both been born in Hampshire. His mother Emily was not recorded on the census return, although the household also included a Cook and a Nurse and a visiting clergyman. The 1911 Census revealed twenty-three-year-old Arthur living at Lillington Rectory, Sherborne, Dorset with his father, fourteen-year-old sister Joan and two domestic servants. The return recorded that Arthur senior had been married for twenty-four years, but again there was no mention of Arthur's mother.

Arthur attended Keble College, Oxford entering in the Michaelmas Term of 1913. He was a member of 1st Hockey XI, 1913 – 1914 and played hockey for Dorset. He was also a member of the University Contingent of the Officers' Training Corp. and was gazetted 2nd Lieutenant in the 1/4th Dorsetshire Regiment in 1915 and promoted to Lieutenant the following year.

Keble College Oxford Students 1913

After service and rigorous training in India the 1/4th Dorsetshire Regiment landed at Basra in late February 1916 as part of 15th Indian Division. A strenuous twelve-day desert march took them to Nasiriyeh, which became their base. Arthur served with the Indian Expeditionary Force from February 1916 but was sadly killed in action at Ramadi on 29 September 1917 and buried at Ramadi Ridge. He was twenty-nine years of age.

The first Battle of Ramadi (west of Baghdad, in present-day Iraq) had lasted five days from 8–13 July 1917 and resulted in an Ottoman victory. The temperatures had soared and were several degrees higher in tents and dug-outs, making it impossible to march even at night. On 8 July, the British moved against Ramadi, using 127 Ford vans to ferry infantry forward. The presumption of senior British officers was that the Turkish garrison would withdraw from the town rather than fight. But this was not the case. The British cavalry got to the west of Ramadi but the infantry, now on foot, were held up by a canal and enemy artillery fire. A dust storm blew in interfering with British communications and artillery observation. Casualties mounted and heat exhaustion added to the evacuations needed, the temperature taken that day in Baghdad being 160 degrees in the sun. Having lost 566 men, 321 of them to heat exhaustion, the British withdrew that night under cover of darkness to the river bank, totally incapable of further efforts with men dying of thirst or heat-stroke. The next day the British withdrew down the river, being harried by Arab horsemen who sniped and killed stragglers. A big lesson had been learned about taking offensive action during the summer months.

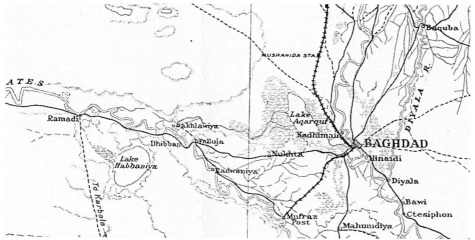

Map of the Euphrates from Ramadi to Baghdad in 1917

The second, ultimately successful British effort to take Ramadi was mounted on 28–29 September 1917 (1 day). The Turks expected an attack to come up the river bank and they had sited their defences accordingly. The Turks in Ramadi had 3,500 infantrymen, 500 cavalrymen and 500 artillerymen with 10 guns. The British attacked with Major General Sir H T Brooking's 15th Division. The divisional strength was over 15,000 men and for the attack the 6th Cavalry Brigade and the 12th and 42nd Infantry Brigades (which included the 1/4th Dorsets 1/5th, 2/5th and 2/6th Gurkhas, the 130th Machine Gun Company and the 448th Field Company Royal Engineers.) were used. Over 40 guns and howitzers were available with support from 'B' Flight 30th Squadron Royal Flying Corps, four armoured cars of the 13th Light Armoured Motor Battery, engineers, pioneers, three portable wireless stations and the Ford light vans. At 1300 hours the 1/5th and 2/5th Gurkhas were ordered to advance together on Ramadi Ridge with the 1/4th Dorsets in support. 2/6th Gurkhas remained behind as the Brigade reserve. 1/5th Gurkhas moved off at 1310 hours but 2/5th Gurkhas was heavily involved in fighting off hostile Arab irregular troops and did not move until 1400 hours. 1/4th Dorsets sent two companies to assist 2/5th Gurkhas and then advanced behind 1/5th Gurkhas. The 1/5th Gurkhas were on top of the ridge by 1335 hours but quickly took over 100 casualties. By 14.15 hours Major Lawrence Lamonby (see footnote) had led two of his companies forward to fill in gaps on the ridge and the unit war diary states that this is when the heaviest casualties were taken. Shortly afterwards 2/5th Gurkhas arrived and extended the British line, followed by a third Dorset company. At 1600 hours the 2/6th Gurkhas came up and extended the line to the right from the ridge to the canal.

The Turkish troops finally surrendered with 120 men killed in battle and another 190 wounded. 3,456 prisoners, including 145 officers, 13 guns, 12 machine guns, 2 armoured launches, 2 barges and large quantities of arms, ammunition and stores were captured by the British. A handful of members of the garrison escaped by swimming the Euphrates. The capture of Ramadi led to the local Arab tribes switching sides and supporting the British.

Captured Turkish Artillery Piece

Turkish prisoners of war after General Brooking's victory at Ramadi, September 1917.

Following Arthur's death Brigadier General F G Lucas wrote: 'He was a most promising officer and would have certainly risen had he remained in the Army. He set a splendid example to the men. I mourn you with the loss of a brave and lovable gentlemen' and Major A Lamonby; 'His constant cheerfulness made him a favourite with all in the mess'. His Commanding Officer, Captain P A Plincke, also wrote: 'He led his platoon on with great dash and gallantry, and I have reported on him accordingly.' He was a good athlete and distinguished himself in all his schools, more particularly at hockey and football. He played several seasons at hockey for his university and for his country. (Extract from De Ruvigny's Roll of Honour).

He is remembered at Baghdad (North Gate) War Cemetery Part II in Iraq. The North Gate Cemetery was begun In April 1917 and has been greatly enlarged since the end of the First World War by graves brought in from other burial grounds in Baghdad and northern Iraq, and from battlefields and cemeteries in Anatolia where Commonwealth prisoners of war were buried by the Turks. At present, 4,160 Commonwealth casualties of the First World War are commemorated by name in the cemetery, many of them on special memorials. Unidentified burials from this period number 2,729. Arthur is also remembered in St Martin's Church, Lillington, Dorset where his father was Rector from 1907 until 1913.

ARTHUR HAMILTON WINTHROP WOODRUFF
LIEUT. 4TH DORSETS.
KILLED IN ACTION AT RAMADIE
25TH SEPT. 1917.
AGED 29.
ELDER SON OF MR A.W. WOODRUFF AND THE
REVᵈ A.W. WOODRUFF, RECTOR OF LILLINGTON, 1907-13.

Memorial Plaque Arthur Hamilton Winthrop Woodruff

Footnote:

Distinguished Service Order: For his gallant leadership during the battle for Ramadi Major Lawrence Lamonby, 1/4th Border Regiment attached to the 1/4th Dorsetshire Regiment, was awarded a Distinguished Service Order. His citation in the London Gazette dated 11 January 1919 read:

For conspicuous gallantry and devotion to duty. He commanded his battalion with great coolness and ability under heavy fire. His initiative and dash enabled the attack to be carried through to a successful conclusion.

LESLIE WOODS and The Military Cross

Leslie was born in Hackney in 1892 and as a young boy attended a small boarding school there. His father William was a Manufacturer's Agent (Furniture) born in Dublin whilst his mother Rosaline was a Londoner born in Kennington. The 1911 Census revealed that the couple had been married for twenty-three years and that nineteen-year-old Leslie, an Apprentice Engineer, was their only son. The family lived at The Salt Box, in Fetcham.

Leslie served in the Royal Field Artillery, 15th Divisional Ammunition Column and held the rank of Lieutenant (Acting Captain).

Medal Card for Leslie Woods

Royal Field Artillery Gunners

Ammunition Columns, Brigade or Divisional, were officered and manned by the Royal Artillery. Intended for direct affiliation to their Brigades, and Divisions, they were additionally called upon to furnish ammunition to any unit requiring it during an action. The Officers and Gunners of the Royal Artillery employed with an Ammunition Column were, as a matter of course, immediately available to replace casualties in the batteries. Working mostly at night, moving forward, the Brigade Ammunition Columns ammunition wagons were interchangeable with a Firing Batteries own ammunition wagons (one per gun), so full wagons could be easily 'dropped-off', being unhooked and taken away for reloading.

Leslie lost his life on the 25 February 1919 aged twenty-seven and is remembered both at the Halle Communal Cemetery, Belgium and at Fetcham War Memorial and St Mary's Churchyard.

Halle Communal Cemetery, Belgium

He was awarded the Military Cross and the announcement appeared in The London Gazette of 3 June 1919. The Military Cross was awarded for an act or acts of exemplary gallantry during active operations against the enemy on land, to captains or officers of lower rank up to warrant officers and was first established by King George V on 28 December 1914

The Leslie Woods Memorial in St Mary's Churchyard, Fetcham.

6836 Supplement to The London Gazette, 3 June, 1919. Awarded the Military Cross Lt. (A./Capt.) Leslie Woods, R.F.A., S.R., Attd: 15th, D.A.C.

The Military Cross

WOODS Leslie of The Salt Box Fetcham Leatherhead **Surrey** captain R.F.A. died 25 February 1919 in Belgium Administration **London** 7 February to William Henry Woods manufacturer's agent. Effects £184 8s. 10d.

Probate was granted on 7 February 1920 and Leslie's estate was left to his father William.

Leslie's father William Woods applied to Epsom Rural District Council in October 1919, on behalf of several Fetcham residents, for consent to the erection of a Memorial Cross at the junction of River Lane and Stoke Road.

FREDERICK WORSFOLD

Frederick was born in Oxshott in 1892 and in 1901 lived with his parents John and Emma at Woodlands Park Kennels, his father John being employed as an agricultural worker. By 1911 Frederick was boarding with Albert Brunger at Fetcham Park, where both were employed as gardeners.

With the outbreak of World War One he enlisted with The Coldstream Guards, Regimental Number 12582 entering the theatre of war in August 1915. He died in December 1917 and according to his Medal Card was posthumously awarded the 1915 Star, Victory and British Medals. Under 'Remarks' the wording 'D of W' was inscribed referring to the fact that he had died of the wounds inflicted.

Fetcham Park

Medal Card

In 1915, the 1st battalion were in action during The Battle of Aubers, transferring on 25 August to 2nd Guards Brigade, Guards Division and were in action in The Battle of Loos. During 1916, they fought on The Somme in The Battle of Flers-Courcelette and The Battle of Morval, capturing Lesboeufs. In 1917, they saw action in the German retreat to the Hindenburg Line, the Third Battle of Ypres and The Battle of Cambrai.

According to a newspaper article Frederick was reported missing on 17 November, when the battalion was on the march, and died of wounds on 4 December aged twenty-five. He is remembered at Valenciennes (St Roch) Communal Cemetery in France Grave/Memorial Reference: IV. E. 26.

The *Surrey Advertiser* 10 April 1918 reported his death as follows: *'Corporal Frederick Worsfold, 1st Battalion Coldstream Guards, only son of Mr J and Mrs Worsfold, Payne's Green, Ockley, aged 25, died of wounds in a German field hospital at Valenciennes, France on December 4, 1917 and was buried in the cemetery at Valenciennes. He was previously reported missing on November 17, 1917. Joining up in August 1914 he had been wounded twice. He worked at Fetcham Park before the war'.*

Valenciennes (St Roch) Communal Cemetery

CHAPTER EIGHT

LETTERS HOME AND IN THE LOCAL NEWSPAPERS

JAMES WILLIAM HIGGS

James was born in Mickleham in 1888 and was the only son of William and Mary Higgs. As a two year, old he lived with his parents at Woodlands, in Leatherhead. His twenty-seven-year-old father was a gardener domestic. By the 1891 census the family had moved to Fetcham Park Lodge. Some twenty years later in 1911 James, now described as a schoolmaster, was lodging with two other young schoolmasters with a family in Brixton.

An article appeared in the *Surrey Mirror* of 2 April 1915 under the title 'Gibraltar - Impressions of a Fetcham Man' and referred to an interesting letter received by Mr Knowles, the schoolmaster, from one of his old boys,' Corpl Higgs' who was out in Gibraltar. The following are extracts from this article:

'After an exceeding rough voyage, we sighted Gibraltar on Sunday morning, after being on board for a week. It was a grand sight as we gradually entered the Strait; the sun was shining brilliantly, on the left, away to the north, the snow-capped mountains of the Sierra Nevada stood out conspicuously against the deep blue sky, while on the opposite side the African coast provided an interesting spectacle. Here and there on the Spanish coast small towns and villages could be seen nestling among the hills, the white buildings, affording a pleasant contrast to the undulating hills of a brownish green colour. The sea, too, was of a very brilliant blue, not to be associated with the water around our own shores. By degrees the Rock loomed up in the distance, appearing to us like a huge lion in a crouching position, with head erect'. 'As the ship approached, one could distinguish the town with its splendid harbour lying at the foot of the rock on the western side. On landing, the stranger usually recognises that he has erred a great deal in his previous ideas of the place. He imagined Gibraltar to be more or less a barren rock, important because of its position on the map; its coaling station, and its harbour. His surprise is therefore great when he discovers a seaport town of some 26,000 inhabitants, flanked by country which is by no means desolate or barren. The local flora is exceeding rich and varied, and trees have been planted in great numbers. The clematis, geranium, aloe and rose run wild, and the myrtle, locust tree, the wide spreading bella sombre, a great variety of cactus, the vine, fig trees, olive, almond, orange and lemon are present in various localities'.

'The town or city (it has a cathedral) consists of two distinct portions, known as north and south, the former being by far the most important'. 'The general character of the climate is very agreeable from November to May, but the remaining five months are hot, and the east wind or Levanter prevails'. ' When a north wind blows in Winter, which is rather uncommon, it is often bitterly cold, from passing over the snows of the Sierra Nevada on its route, but no great extreme cold is ever known. The Levanter is most unwholesome, it is usually accompanied by a dense mass of dark cloud, which hangs over the Rock and dissolves into clammy and unpleasant moisture. Living as we do at Europa Point, on the extreme south, we miss for the most part the ill-effects of the Levanter. When the town is hot and extremely close, Europa is breezy and pleasant'

'The general health of people resident upon the Rock now compares favourably with many towns in England. This is satisfactory, more especially when this is taken into consideration the fact that the houses are closely packed together'. 'Rock fever, as it was locally called, has almost entirely disappeared, the general health of the troops is excellent.'

'Government House, the official residence of the Governor, and formerly a convent, is a plain but spacious and commodious building with good reception rooms. In the summer, the Governor lives at 'The Cottage' a long straggling building on the Mediterranean side'. 'The Military Hospital is a very fine building occupying a commanding site upon a plateau and having accommodation for 206 patients'. 'There is a theatre capable of seating 1,000 persons. Here Spanish Opera may be seen (of a sort) for a very modest sum.' 'By far the most interesting relic of antiquity in Gibraltar is the Moorish Castle, certainly more than 1,150 years old. A great deal of it is still standing, though sadly disfigured by modern buildings'. 'The harbour is one of the finest in the world, and is said to be second only to Sydney. Here the shipping of all nations may be seen (including German!), the great 'Queen Elizabeth' was here for many days before proceeding east. Battleships are always coming and going, while at night some dozen searchlights illuminate the Straits for miles around.'

The Duke of Cambridge's Own (Middlesex Regiment 2/7th Battalion was formed at Hornsey in September 1914 as a second line unit. It moved to Barnet and then Egham, where it was attached to 2/Middlesex Brigade (201st), 2/Home Counties Division (67th). It left the Division in February 1915 and moved to Gibraltar, moving again in August 1915 to Egypt and where it formed part of the Western Frontier Force. In May 1916 it moved to France, arriving Marseilles on 15 May 1916 and the whole Battalion went into quarantine camp for Typhus.

The Duke of Cambridge's Own (Middlesex Regiment).

The undermentioned Serjeants to be Second Lieutenants. Dated 11th January, 1916:—

James William Higgs.
George Arthur Scutt.

A further article in the *Dorking and Leatherhead Advertiser* of 4 March 1916 reported James's promotion: 'The many friends of Mr J W Higgs, only son of Mr and Mrs Higgs, The Lodge, Fetcham Park will be pleased to hear that he has received a commission for his own regiment, the 2/7th Middlesex. Lieut. Higgs, who is well known locally, held an important appointment under the London School and at the outbreak of war enlisted as a private in the 2/7th Middlesex. He soon gained promotion, and held a rank of sergeant when he was gazetted Lieutenant. After his preliminary training in England, Lieut. Higgs was stationed at Gibraltar for six months and during the past seven months he has seen active service in Egypt, where his regiment has been engaged with the Senussi Arabs. The high esteem in which Lieut. Higgs is held by the officers of the 2/7th Middlesex is shown by the fact that he should take up his commission in the regiment with which he had been associated since the outbreak of the war.'

James was mentioned again in the The London Gazette dated 17 October 1916

Middlesex Regt.—2nd Lt. J. W. Higgs is seconded for duty with Trench Mortar Battery. 14th Sept. 1916.

In November of 1916 James married Amy Elsie Pearman at the Parish Church in Epsom and his profession was described at 2nd Lieutenant. He gave his address as Fetcham Park Lodge

The London Gazette of 18 February 1916 referred to James's promotion from Sergeant to Lieutenant.

COMMISSION FOR FETCHAM RESIDENT.

LIEUT. J. W. HIGGS.

	When Married.	Name and Surname.	Age.	Condition.	Rank or Profession.	Residence at the time of Marriage	Father's Name and Surname.	Rank or Profession of Father.
66	20 Nov 1916	James William Higgs	28	Bachelor	Lieutenant	Fetcham Park Lodge Fetcham	James William Higgs	Gardener
		Amy Elsie Pearman	28	Spinster		3 Heathcote Villas Epsom		

1916. Marriage solemnized at The Parish Church in the Parish of Epsom in the County of Surrey

Married in the Parish Church according to the Rites and Ceremonies of the Church of England by or after Banns me A P Metcalfe

This Marriage was solemnized between us { James William Higgs / Amy Elsie Pearman } in the Presence of us { Charlie J Pearman / Jean Papa Pearman / A Childs }

115

First name	James William
Last name	Higgs
Rank	Captain
Unit or regiment	Middlesex Rgt; Trench Mortars; Intelligence Corp
LCC dept	Education Officer's Department
LCC section	Teaching Staff
Theatre	Gibraltar 6 months; Egypt 9 months; France 8 months; North Russia 12 months
War service from	1914
War service to	1919
Record set	London County Council Record of war Service 1914-1918
Country	England
Category	Military, armed forces & conflict
Subcategory	First World War
Collections from	Great Britain

The London County Council published the list in a book in 1920 that was presented to every person listed (and to the next of kin when that serviceman or woman was killed). The information from the London County Council Record of Service was published in two parts: a narrative of the war and a published roll of men sorted by the department they worked in.

James's father was to pass away in June 1949 in Trimmers Cottage Hospital in Farnham, leaving his estate of £1,413 to James who was referred to as a retired schoolmaster.

Whilst James Higgs wrote a long and descriptive letter home to his old school master, many soldiers sent home postcards to their loved ones, embroidered cards being especially popular. The pencilled message on the reverse was often very brief, but nonetheless poignant. One card 'To the Dear Ones at Home' bore the message 'From your loving husband who is always thinking of you'.

Silk postcard 'To the Dear Ones at Home'

Another card sent in 1917 from France and again embroidered in silk just carried the words 'From your loving husband Jim'.

Similar postcards sending birthday and Christmas greetings from wives and children were sent out from Britain to the troops. One read 'Loving Birthday Greetings to Dear Dad on Active Service' and carried the verse:

'Dear Dad, I send my wishes fond,
To greet you on your Birthday morn,
And hope before its glad return
That brighter, happier days may dawn
When victory shall bless our arms
The battle ours, the fighting o'er
With peace to banish war's alarms
And bring you safely home once more.'

116

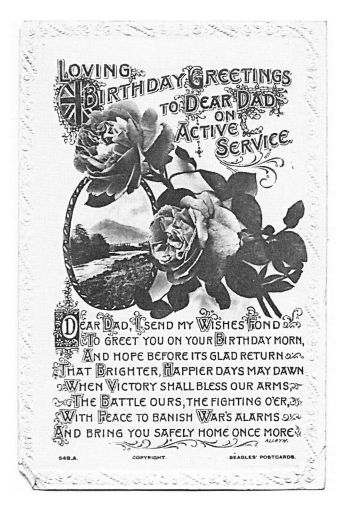

Birthday Greetings to Dear Dad

Postcard 'For my Daddy'.

This photograph of soldiers sorting mail at a field post office December 1914.

The Postal Section proved a thoroughly organised department of the British Field Force, and worked with remarkable smoothness and promptness, so that the men in the fighting line had little to complain about in the delivery of the letters sent to them by their friends or of delay in their own letters home.

The following article appeared in the *Surrey Advertiser* of 20 February 1915:

'JUST LIKE SURREY'
FETCHAM MAN'S INTERESTING LETTER

A member of the Honourable Artillery Company, whose home is in Fetcham, Surrey, frequently refers in his letters to the similarity of the scenery in Belgium to that round his home. In his last letter, he says:-

'We are now nearly through our third day in case billets and trenches, and tomorrow morning will be going down for another four days' rest if all's well. We had to shift our position last night, and I had a rum job getting all my belongings together: but here I am, within three-quarters of a mile of the Bosches, with our guns going off all round and the rifles in the distance.

The weather has been glorious for the last few days, and yesterday morning I had a little walk round some fields in the sunshine. Some kiddies were playing round a farm, and the birds singing cheerily; not a rifle or gun to be heard. The view was glorious. It made one forget for a few moments that there was a war on at all.

When I was standing in the hills yesterday I could just imagine that I was on Fetcham Downs, looking over towards Bookham Common. If one was just above Roaring House Farm, the trenches would be about on the Lower Bookham Road, so you can guess we were not far off. We had one corporal killed and four or five men wounded yesterday.'

Another article appeared in the *Surrey Advertiser* of 17 April 1915, presumably from the same source:

'Co-operation in Belgium'
FETCHAM MAN'S OBSERVATIONS

'A member of the Honourable Artillery Company, who hails from Fetcham and is now serving in the trenches in Belgium, in a letter to relatives makes some interesting observations upon agricultural co-operation as carried out in that country, even under present difficulties. He says:-

'Our billet is a little general shop, the proprietor of which is the Government meat inspector, and manager of the local creamery. His wife and two young daughters attend to the shop. They are very nice people, some of the best we have struck so far. It will be most interesting, when the war is over, to make a tour round all the villages we have been through and meet the different people with whom we have been billeted (some clean and some very dirty).

In every village of any size they have a creamery, where all the farmers in the district (who are shareholders) take their eggs and milk. These creameries separate the milk, make the butter, sort and pack eggs, rabbits, etc. which are sold to French and English merchants.

This form of co-operation seems to be employed extensively out here. Sugar beet and tobacco are also dealt with in the same way, and no doubt it renders a better profit than if sold by the individual grower. I cannot understand why this system should not be adopted by English farmers.'

CHAPTER NINE

PEACE CELEBRATIONS AND AFTER THE WAR

Armistice Day 11 November 1918 Day was officially the last day of World War although on many parts of the Western Front fighting continued as normal and casualties were inflicted at the same time as celebrations at home were taking place. The Armistice was an agreement signed by representatives of France, Great Britain and Germany to end fighting as a prelude to peace negotiations. The Treaty of Versailles signed six months later would act as the peace treaty between the nations.

Daily Telegraph 'World War is Over' 11 November 1918

Sadly, the country was still in the grips of Spanish Influenza which would claim thousands of lives worldwide.

The following summer on 19 July 1919 a public holiday to celebrate peace was declared and thousands gathered in London, having arrived overnight. Nearly 15,000 troops took part in the victory parade, led by Allied commanders Haig (British commander in chief) Foch (Allied Supreme Commander) and Pershing (Head of the US Expeditionary Force), who saluted fallen comrades.

King George V issued a message: 'To these, the sick and wounded who cannot take part in the festival of victory, I send out greetings and bid them good cheer, assuring them that the wounds and scars so honourable in themselves, inspire in the hearts of their fellow countrymen the warmest feelings of gratitude and respect.'

Crowds gathering outside Buckingham Palace Peace Celebrations July 1919

A monument to those killed and wounded was unveiled in Whitehall, to mark the end point of the victory parade, and was later decorated with flower wreaths.

Victory Parade in Whitehall, London on 19 July 1919

The first cenotaph was a wood-and-plaster structure designed by Sir Edwin Lutyens. It was one of a number of temporary structures erected for the London Victory Parade (also called the Peace Day Parade) in July 1919. The British War Cabinet decided on 30 July 1919 that a permanent memorial should replace the wooden version and be designated Britain's official national war memorial. The announcement was made on 23 October 1919 that the Portland stone version would be a *'replica exact in every detail in permanent material of present temporary structure'.*

Thousands of celebrations took place in towns and villages around the country including a parade in Leatherhead and celebrations in Fetcham. The school log book recorded the event as follows: '19 July (Saturday) Celebrations of Peace throughout the country took the form of a procession in fancy dress round the lanes at 3 pm, tea and sports for the children at 4 pm, a dinner for returned soldiers at 6 pm and a dance in the school room (owing to the rain) at 7 pm'.

Peace Parade in Leatherhead July 1919

School Log Book 19 July 1919

APPENDIX

COLONEL HANKEY

Gheluvelt (31 October 1914)

In 1914, the Germans invaded France. Their aim was to overwhelm the French and British Armies, bypass Paris and seize the Channel Ports. Only the British Army remained, at Ypres, to stem the advancing Germans and save the Channel Ports and Paris.

The crisis of the Battle of Ypres hinged around the village of Gheluvelt. Lying on a forward spur of the low ridge that covers the town of Ypres, Gheluvelt was the last point retained in British hands from which the enemy's line could be dominated.

On the evening of 30th October, the Second Battalion The Worcestershire Regiment remained uncommitted, all other units having been sent to reinforce the line. Located in Polygon Wood, the Battalion, was commanded by Major E B Hankey and the Adjutant was Captain B C Senhouse-Clarke. At 13.00 hours on 31 October, the Battalion received an order to attack and retake Gheluvelt. Captain A F Thorne of the Grenadier Guards was to act as a guide. From Polygon Wood, the chateau which dominated the village could not be seen but the nearby church tower rising amidst the smoke, was visible. All around were wounded and stragglers coming to the rear and batteries could be seen limbering up and moving back. The Worcestershires alone were moving towards the enemy. The ridge was littered with dead and wounded, and along the crest, German shells were falling fast. Hankey decided that the only way to cross this dangerous area was at the double. As the leading men reached the ridge, they came in view of the German guns whose high explosive shells were quickly directed on the charging soldiers. Over 100 of the Battalion were killed or wounded but the rest pushed on and, increasing their speed as they came to the downward slope in sight of Gheluvelt, made the final charge through hedges and on to the Chateau grounds. Here they met the remnants of the South Wales Borderers who had made a heroic stand. The meeting was unexpected, for the Worcestershires had believed no soldiers were left. The 2nd Worcestershires had gone into this action with about 370 men of whom 187 were killed or wounded. Gheluvelt had been saved and the line restored. It is rare that the action of one unit can exert such a profound influence as did this now famous counter attack.

THE BATTLE OF GHELUVELT (2nd Battalion Worcestershire Regiment) – War Diaries)

Daybreak of October 31st was calm and clear. The 2nd Worcestershire, in their reserve position west of the Polygon Wood, were roused early by the crash of gun-fire. The troops turned out, breakfasts were cooked and eaten, weapons were cleaned and inspected. Then for several hours the companies lay idle about their billets, listening to the ever-increasing bombardment and watching the German shrapnel bursting in black puffs of smoke above the tree-tops.

The 2nd Worcestershire were almost the last available reserve of the British defence. Nearly every other unit had been drawn into the battle-line or had been broken beyond recovery; and to an onlooker that last reserve would not have seemed very formidable. The Battalion could muster not more than five hundred men. Ten days of battle had left all ranks haggard, unshaven and unwashed: their uniforms had been soaked in the mud of the Langemarck trenches and torn by the brambles of Polygon Wood: many had lost their puttees or their caps. But their weapons were clean and in good order, they had plenty of ammunition, and three months of war had given them confidence in their fighting power. The short period in reserve had allowed them sleep and food. That crowd of ragged soldiers was still a fighting battalion, officers and men bound together by that proud and willing discipline which is the soul of the Regiment.

Hour by hour the thunder of the guns grew more intense. Stragglers and wounded from beyond the wood brought news that a great German attack was in progress. The enemy's infantry were coming on in overwhelming numbers against the remnants of the five British battalions, together mustering barely a thousand men, which were holding the trenches about the Menin Road.

Before midday weight of numbers had told. The Queen's and the Royal Scots Fusiliers had fought to the last, the Welsh and the KRRC had been overwhelmed, the right flank of the South Wales Borderers had been rolled back. Gheluvelt had been lost, and a great gap had been broken in the British line. Unless that gap could be closed the British army was doomed to disaster.

So serious was the situation caused by the loss of Gheluvelt that orders were issued for the British artillery to move back, in preparation for a general retreat, At the same time it was decided that a counter-attack against the lost position should be made by the 2nd Worcestershire Brigadier-General C FitzClarence, VC (Commanding the 1st (Guards) Brigade. Technically the 2nd Worcestershire, belonging to the 2nd Division, were not under his orders. General Lomax, commanding the 1st Division, had directed General FitzClarence to order the Worcestershire into the fight), was in command of the front about the Menin Road. Soon after midday he sent for an officer of the 2nd Worcestershire to take orders. Major Hankey sent his Adjutant, Captain B C Senhouse Clarke.

Twenty minutes later Captain Senhouse Clarke returned, bringing word that the Battalion would probably be wanted for a counter-attack, and that meanwhile one company was to be detached to prevent the enemy from advancing up the Menin Road. 'A' Company was detailed for the latter duty. Led by Captain P S G Wainman, the company advanced at 12.45 pm (the other officers of ' A ' Coy. were Lieut. E C R Hudson and 2/Lieut. G A Sheppard) to a position on the embankment of the light railway northwest of Gheluvelt. The company held the embankment during the following two hours, firing rapidly at such of the enemy as attempted to advance beyond the houses.

About 1 pm, Major Hankey was summoned by General FitzClarence, and was given definite orders. The 2nd Worcestershire were to make a counter-attack to regain the lost British positions around Gheluvelt. General FitzClarence pointed out the Church in Gheluvelt as a landmark for the advance, explained that the situation was desperate and that speed was essential, and ordered his Staff Captain, Captain A F Thorne of the Grenadier Guards, to guide the Battalion on its way.

At 1.45pm Major Hankey sent off the Battalion scouts, under Lieutenant E A Haskett-Smith, to cut any wire fences across the line of advance. Extra ammunition was issued, and all kit was lightened as much as possible, packs being left behind. Then bayonets were fixed, and at 2pm the Battalion moved off in file, led by Major Hankey and Captain Thorne, along under cover of the trees to the south-west corner of Polygon Wood (Afterwards known as ' Black Watch Corner.').

From that corner of the wood the ground to the south-eastward is clear and open, falling to the little valley of the Reutelbeek and rising again to the bare ridge above Polderhoek. That ridge hid from view the Chateau of Gheluvelt, and the exact situation there was unknown; but further to the right could be seen the Church tower rising amid the smoke of the burning village.

The open ground was dotted with wounded and stragglers coming back from the front. In every direction German shells were bursting. British batteries could be seen limbering up and moving to the rear. Everywhere there were signs of retreat. The Worcestershire alone were moving towards the enemy. But the three companies tramped grimly forward, down into the valley of the Reutelbeek.

Beyond a little wood the Battalion deployed, 'C' and 'D' Companies in front line, with 'B' Company in second line behind about 370 all told (Including eight officers Major E B Hankey (commanding), Captain B C Senhouse Clarke (Adjutant), Captain E L Bowring, Captain H C Grimley, 2/Lieut. F C F Biscoe ('C' Coy.), Captain R J Ford ('D' Coy.), Captain E G Williams ('B' Coy.) and 2/Lieut. C H Ralston. Lieut. E A Haskett-Smith, the Battalion Scout Officer, had preceded the three companies). In front of them rose the bare slope of the Polderhoek ridge. The ridge was littered with dead and wounded, and along its crest the enemy's shells were bursting in rapid succession. Major Hankey decided that the only way of crossing that deadly stretch of ground was by one long rush. The companies extended into line and advanced.

The ground underfoot was rank grass or rough stubble. The two leading companies broke into a steady double and swept forward across the open, the officers leading on in front, and behind them their men with fixed bayonets in one long irregular line. As they reached the crest, the rushing wave of bayonets was sighted by the hostile artillery beyond. A storm of shells burst along the ridge. Shrapnel bullets rained down and high-explosive shells crashed into the charging line. Men fell at every pace: over a hundred of the Battalion were killed or wounded: the rest dashed on. The speed of the rush increased as on the downward slope the troops came in sight of Gheluvelt Chateau close in front. The platoons scrambled across the light railway, through some hedges and wire fences, and then in the grounds of the Chateau they closed with the enemy.

The enemy were ill-prepared to meet the charge. The German infantry were crowded in disorder among the trees of the park, their attention divided between exploring the out-houses and surrounding the remnant of the British defenders; for the musketry of the defence still swept the lawn in front of the Chateau. The enemy's disorder was increased by a sharp and accurate fire of shrapnel from British batteries behind Polygon Wood.

The Germans were young troops of newly-formed units (The 244th and 245th Reserve Regiments and the 16th Bavarian Reserve Regiment). Probably they had lost their best leaders earlier in the day, for they made no great attempt to stand their ground and face the counter-attack. They gave way at once before the onslaught of the British battalion and crowded back out of the grounds of the Chateau into the hedgerows beyond. Shooting and stabbing, 'C' Company ('C' Company were led by Captain E L Bowring, closely followed by 2/Lieut. F C F Biscoe) of the Worcestershire charged across the lawn and came up into line with the gallant remnant of the South Wales Borderers.

The South Wales Borderers had made a wonderful stand. All day they had held their ground at the Chateau and they were still stubbornly fighting although almost surrounded by the enemy. Their resistance had delayed and diverted the German advance, and the success of the counter-attack was largely due to their brave defence.

The meeting of the two battalions was unexpected. The Worcestershire had not known that any of the South Wales Borderers were still holding out. Major Hankey went over to their commander and found him to be Colonel H E Burleigh Leach, an old friend. With him was their second-in-command Major A J Reddie, brother of Major J M. Reddie of the Worcestershire. 'My God, fancy meeting you here,' said Major Hankey, and Colonel Burleigh Leach replied quietly 'Thank God you have come.'

The routed enemy were hunted out of the hedges (Among those specially distinguished for gallantry in that fighting were Sergts. G Ellis and A E Kemp : both received the DCM) and across the open fields beyond the Chateau. 'C' and 'D' Companies of the Worcestershire took up position in the sunken road, which runs past the grounds. 'B' Company was brought up and prolonged the line to the right.

But the village of Gheluvelt, on the slope above the right flank, was still in the enemy's hands. Most of the German troops in the village seem to have been drawn northwards by the fighting around the Chateau; but a certain number of Saxons of the 242nd Regiment had remained in the village, whence they opened a fire which took the sunken road in enfilade. To silence that fire Major Hankey sent fighting patrols from the front line into the village. Those patrols drove back the German snipers and took some prisoners (In that fighting Sergt. P Sutton showed great bravery. Attacking a German machine-gun single-handed he captured one of its team and put the gun out of action. Sergt. Sutton was subsequently awarded the DCM. During that patrol fighting in the village, Lieut. Haskett-Smith was severely wounded and Sergt. G F Poole was killed): but it became clear that the position in the sunken road would be unsafe until the village was secured. Accordingly Major Hankey sent orders to Captain Wainman that 'A' Company were to advance from their defensive position and occupy the village. Captain Wainman led forward his company and, after some sharp fighting among burning buildings and bursting shells, occupied a new line with his left flank in touch with the right of the position in the sunken road and his right flank in the village, holding the church and churchyard. Thence he sent forward patrols to clear the village. Those patrols, led by a tall young subaltern, 2nd Lieutenant G A Sheppard, worked forward from house to house till they reached the cross-roads at the eastern end of Gheluvelt. It was not possible permanently to occupy the centre of the village, for it was being bombarded by both the German and the British artillery. On all sides houses were burning, roofs falling and walls collapsing. The stubborn Saxons still held some small posts in the scattered houses on the south-eastern outskirts. Nevertheless the enemy's main force had been driven out, and the peril of a collapse of the British defence about the Menin Road had been averted.

The German forces made no further effort that day to retake Gheluvelt. The reason for the enemy's inaction is not clear. It is possible that the very boldness of the counter-attack may have given the impression that the Battalion was but the first wave of a stronger force, and possibly the enemy may have stood on the defensive to meet that imagined attack. Furthermore, the British artillery maintained throughout the afternoon a heavy fire on the low ground east of Gheluvelt, a fire which may have disorganised the enemy and which probably hampered the transmission of information and orders : indeed, the vagueness of most German accounts of the fighting at Gheluvelt suggests that the position in the village was not ascertained. In such circumstances, with the situation obscure, young troops discouraged and hostile shell-fire unsubdued, it is no easy matter to organise a fresh attack. Perhaps some commander of importance was disabled or some vital line of communication severed. Whatever the reason, the result was that the enemy's action during the rest of the day was limited to a violent bombardment, which fortunately caused but little loss. The 2nd Worcestershire held firm on the ground they had won, 'while behind them General Fitz-Clarence reorganised his troops and made preparations for further resistance.

Evening came on. From his position in the village Captain Wainman sent out patrols to the right to gain touch with any troops who might be there. But no communication with any other unit could be established, nor did any other British troops come forward to the position held by the Battalion.

About 6pm came fresh orders from General Fitz-Clarence. The General had decided to withdraw his defensive line from the forward slope of the ridge at Gheluvelt to a new position further back at Veldhoek where the trenches would be sheltered from direct observation of the German artillery.

The order was sent along the line. Arrangements were made in conjunction with the South Wales Borderers and the retirement was begun. One by one, at intervals of ten minutes, the companies withdrew from their positions. In the darkness, they assembled under cover and then tramped back along the Menin Road to Veldhoek. The withdrawal was not realised by the enemy, and was carried out without interference, save for the intermittent bombardment which continued throughout that night (The evacuation of Gheluvelt was not discovered by the enemy until dawn next morning (November 1st). Then the village and the Chateau were occupied by the 242nd Reserve Regiment, who drove out a few remaining British stragglers). As the last company of the 2nd Worcestershire marched back out of the village, several of the houses were still burning, and the darkness was torn at intervals by the blaze of bursting shells. Four long years were to pass before the bayonets of the Regiment were again to sweep through the ruins of Gheluvelt.

At Veklhoek the Battalion halted in the darkness, deployed facing east and began to entrench the new position. Presently troops of the 1st Brigade relieved the Worcestershire, and the Battalion drew back into reserve. Officers and men lay down where they halted, and slept the sleep of exhaustion.

The day's fighting had cost the 2nd Worcestershire a third of the Battalion's remaining strength, for 187 of all ranks (including three officers wounded Captain E G Williams, Lieut. E C R Hudson, Lieut. E A Haskett-Smith.) had been killed or wounded; but their achievement had been worthy of that sacrifice. Their counter-attack had thrown back the enemy at a moment, which the British Commander-in-Chief afterwards called 'the worst half-hour of my life.' In all probability that counter-attack had saved Ypres from capture and the British army from defeat. It had been a desperate measure to retrieve a desperate situation; and no one could have foretold its extraordinary success in paralysing the German advance.

That success was not achieved by the 2nd Worcestershire alone. Success would hardly have been possible but for the brave defence of the South Wales Borderers and the supporting fire of the artillery. Nevertheless, it stands to the perpetual credit of the Regiment that at the darkest hour of that great battle, when all others around them were in retreat, our war-worn officers and men went forward unflinching to meet unknown odds, and by their devotion saved the day.

In recognition of the gallantry shown at Polygon Wood and Gheluvelt, the following' awards were made: Major E B Hankey to be Brevet Lt.-Colonel, Captain B C Senhouse Clarke to be Brevet Major. Captain E L Bowring, the DSO, and the MC to Captain R J Ford, Lieut. G A Slaughter and Lieut. E W Carrington, RAMC.

Source: www.worcestershireregiment.com